STRUCTURAL ADJUSTMENT AND IMPLICATION OF HUMAN RIGHTS

STRUCTURAL ADJUSTMENT AND IMPLICATION OF HUMAN RIGHTS

Editors

Prof. G. Saibaba

M.A., Ph.D.

Dean, School of Social and Behavioural Sciences
Coordinator and Head of the Department of
Human Rights and Social Development
Sri Venkateswara University
Tirupati-517 502

&

Dr. K. Sreenivasa Rao

M.A., Ph.D.

Assistant Professor
Department of Human Rights and Social Development
Sri Venkateswara University
Tirupati-517 502

SERIALS PUBLICATIONS

New Delhi

First Published–2003

ISBN: 81-86771-14-X

Published by

Head Office : **SERIALS PUBLICATIONS**
4, B.S.S. Hall, Khyber Pass Market,
Civil Lines, Delhi–110054 (India)
Phone: 0091-11-3811659
Fax: 91-11-3812678
E-mail: serials@satyam.net.in

Branch Office : 4830/24, Prahlad Street, Ansari Road,
Darya Ganj, New Delhi-110002 (India)
Phone: 3245225

Price Rs. : **650/-**

PRINTED IN INDIA

Tarun Offset Printers,

Contents

Editorial Remarks ix

List of Contributors xvii

Part—I

STRUCTURAL ADJUSTMENT AND HUMAN RIGHTS

1. Human Rights: New Challenges in 2001 3
Justice Satyabrata Sinha

2. Impact of Structural Adjustment Policies on the Basic Human Rights of Vulnerable Groups such as Women, Children, Dalits and Tribals 19
Justice P.S. Narayana

3. Structural Adjustment Policy and Human Rights—A Philosophical Analysis 28
A.S. Seetharamu

4. Structural Adjustment Programme (SAP) and Human Rights 44
Prof. D. Narasimha Reddy

5. Structural Imbalances–Courts Role in Strengthening Human Right Jurisprudence 52
Prof. E. Vijaya Kumar

6. Positivisation of Human Rights and Responsibilities–A 21st Century Challenge 61
Prof. A. Lakshminath

7. Human Rights and Judiciary 66
Dr. D. Venkateswarlu

Part—II

HUMAN RIGHTS: LABOUR AND ENVIRONMENT

8. Core Labour Standards, Human Rights and Structural Adjustments: The Indian Experience and Perspectives — 71
Prof. G. Saibaba

9. Institutional Labour Standards on Human Rights—A Review — 97
Dr. K. Uma Devi

10. New Industrial Labour—Insecure Employment, Social Conflict and Labour Rights — 105
G.Vijay

11. Human Rights and Structural Adjustment Programme with Special Reference to Rights of Workers — 134
Mrs. N. Rajeswari

12. Human Right Viewpoint of Environment — 143
Prof. V. Hemalatha Devi & B. Yuvakumar Reddy

13. The Rights and Responsibilities of the Elderly — 150
Prof. P.V. Ramamurti

Part—III

GLOBALISATION; STATE AND HUMAN RIGHTS

14. Globalisation, State and Human Rights — 157
Prof. S. Seshaiah

15. Globalisation, Myth and Reality of Human Rights in India — 163
Prof. (Dr.) Ranbir Singh

16. Right to Development and Globalisation—Paradigm — 170
Prof. P. Prasad

17. Globalisation and its Impact on Human Rights in India 178
Saji Thomas

18. Globalisation, Social Justice with Reference to Right to Health of Women 191
Dr. K. Sreenivasa Rao & Srinivasu

19. Structural Adjustment—And MNCs 204
Smt. P.B. Pankaja

20. Globalisation Reflects and Affects the Rights of Child in India 212
Rayadurgam Narayana

21. SAP Human Rights and Social Justice 223
R.D. Vijayasekhar

22. Empowerment of Agricultural Rural Women Labourers and Human Rights in the Context of Globalisation 229
I. Subramanyam

23. Capital Centric Development-Patriarch Chain of Capital, State and Households—The Question of Unfreedoms 233
Dr. M. Vanamala

EDITORIAL REMARKS

The Department of Human Rights and Social Development has been organising seminars and conferences on contemporary issues. It has been working like a window between the general public and intelligentia within the university. In pursuance of this aim the Department has organised a two day national seminar on the theme *"Structural Adjustment and implications for Human Rights"*, during 16-17, March 2002. Resource persons from the universities, faculty, research scholars and students of Sri Venkateswara University and Shri Padmvathi Mahila Viswa Vidyalayam have actively participated in the programme.

Prof. G. Saibaba, Head and Coordinator, Department of Human Rights and Social Development welcomed the experts, Resource persons and participants of the programme.

Prof. P. Murali, Vice-Chancellor of Sri Venkateswara University said, Indian Industry has failed to upgrade its technology and establish supremacy in the global market though a decade had passed since the new economic policies were introduced. He further said the SAP instead of promoting productively, employment and better income distribution, it had marginalised the sections. The entry of multinational companies into vital sectors has reduced the employment potentials.

Justice Satyabrata Sinha in his paper on *"Human rights* : New *Challenges in 2001"*, emphasised that the movement for

"Human Rights" is part of human history and it is never a lone sojourner. He stressed the role of Supreme Court of India for the protection and promotion of rights of children. His paper analyses the rights of women, prisoners and Human Rights, HIV-AIDS and human rights, refugees and human rights. The author concluded that the world is caught up in economic liberalisation and global market syndrome. There is need for honest appraisal of human rights practices that would go a long way for giving effect to international treaty or convention rights as well as human rights in the constitution.

Delivering keynote address, Justice P.S. Narayana spoke on the impact of SAP on the basic human rights of vulnerable groups. He also expressed concern over women being denied their rights. On the basis of religion, the fate of the woman remained that she was being treated as a second rate citizen. He cautioned courts to 'be slow' in distributing the benefits being conferred on the SCs/STs as the improvement in their condition due to these facilities are not "remarkable". He concluded that it is needless to state the devaluation of currency also is an essential factor which had the impact of sharp price rise of essential commodities. In formulating policies in a welfare state like India, progress should be taken as paramount consideration but should not be at the total deprivation of ordinary human rights of vulnerable sections of the society and maintenance of balance in this regard is essential.

Prof. A.S. Seetharamu, in his paper on *"Structural Adjustment Policy and Human Rights—A Philosophical Analysis"*, stressed the values associated with human rights, not just globalise trade and investments. He advocated the shift in the policy towards economic reforms and globalisation. He has shown the priorities of the world and advocated for a universal human rights for human development.

Prof. D.N. Reddy in the first part of his paper on *"Structural Adjustment Programme and Human Rights"*, highlighted the meaning of the structural programme. The second part of the paper deals with the implications of structural adjustment programme in terms of the livelihood activities, and social consumption of particularly the poor section. The third part deals with the experience of structural development in some of the less developed countries where it has been operated from 1990's. The final part of the paper deals with the nature of intervention contemplated and their inadequacy. He concluded that withdrawal of the state support form the responsibility of promoting inclusive growth results in severe hardships to the poor wherever they are.

Prof. E. Vijayakumar in his paper entitled *"Structural Imbalances—Courts' role in Strengthening Human Rights Jurisprudence"*, highlighted the importance of the courts in standardising the norms to equalise the unequal. To conclude he said state is duty bound to protect the rights of vulnerable groups in the society.

Prof. A. Lakshminath in his paper on *"Positivisation of Human Rights and Responsibilities—A 21st Century Challenge"*, emphasised that it is the judiciary which alone can successfully meet the challenge in positivising the Human Rights and Human Responsibilities.

Prof. D. Venkateswarulu in his paper on *"Human Rights and Judiciary"* rightly emphasised that the legislature, the judiciary and the executive are said to be the three important organs of the state. The ever changing society expects the judiciary to play effective role for the cause of women, children and the poor in the society.

Prof. G. Saibaba in his paper on *"Core Labour Standards, Human Rights and Structural Adjustment Programmes"* argued for the need for the real struggles for promotion and protection of human rights in a democratic system. He has traced real contribution of Prof. A.K. Sen and the idealist leader Mahatma Gandhi. He has drawn the attention on the need for structural adjustment programmes of counter revolution in development thinking as counter revolution has became ideological the basis for SAP. Further, he has drawn the empirical support for his arguments on the face of growing unemployment, emerging regional industrial relations scene, disinvestment policies and the growing opposition for rapid economic reforms. This paper covered the challenges posed by structural changes on these two-core labour standards and human rights. Further, the author argued for the need for policy on vision for this century on national development policies and programmes.

Dr. K. Uma Devi in her paper on *"International labour standards on Human Rights—A Review"*, has made an attempt to review and examine the international standards on human rights. She concluded that in the light of globalisation, liberalisation and privatisation drastic changes have been proposed in the labour standards which are detrimental to the Indian labour.

Mr. G. Vijay in his paper on *"New industrial labour—insecure employment, social conflict and labour rights"*, stressed that industrial relations in undergoing drastic changes specifically in terms of relationship between the employers and employees. The paper is divided into five sections. This first section deals with introduction. The second section deals with the overall trends in the labour market, the third section presents empirical findings of the worst case scenario in the labour markets, the fourth section presents case studies which reflects the social crisis and the crisis of labour rights which new industrial model creates, the fifth section presents some institutions which are dealing with the social crisis and the question of labour rights.

Mrs. N. Rajeswari in her paper on *"Human Rights and Structural Adjustment Programme: with special reference to rights of worker"*, highlighted that the new structural adjustment programme is infringing the rights of workers. Workers face the threat of being stripped off even the basic human dignity and a right to life. Employment apart, they have to live in a world rife with labour inequalities and discrimination. Increasing prices only add fuel to it and causing a lot of problems to workers.

Prof. V. Hemalatha Devi and B. Yuvakumar Reddy in their paper on *"Human Rights Viewpoint of Environment"*, rightly emphasized that human rights are of crucial significance and are basic to human welfare and prosperity. The authors dealt in detail the human rights interface with environment at the international scenario. They also mentioned that the Indian constitution safeguards the environmental issues. Article 21 of the fundamental right ensures life with dignity.

Prof. P.V. Ramamurti, in his paper on *"The Rights and Responsibilities of the elderly"*, rightly stressed the need for protecting the rights of the older persons in the society. He concluded that the national policy for older persons promulgated by the government of India has, in one form or another, incorporated the provision to protect and promote the rights of the older people. He only hoped that these provisions will find light in the future.

Prof. S. Seshaiah, in his paper on *"Globalisation, State and Human Rights"*, remarked that, the structural adjustment programmes, accommodated by India and implemented in the name of new economic policies which are popularly called as liberalisation, privatisation and globalisation (LPG), stands in contradiction to the fundamental rights and directive principles of the state policies (democratic rights). He said the present democracy is tailored to suit the needs of the market economy. He concluded that as a result of structural adjustment programme the nature of state undergoing change form 'social justice' state to 'law and order state' cause greater threat to human rights.

Prof. Ranbir Singh in his paper entitled *"Globalisation: Myth and Reality of Human Rights in India"*, highlighted that W.T.O. regime is affecting the trade in developing countries. The SAP has negative impact on indigenous people. Unfortunately poverty reduction has not taken place in the reform years. He concluded that if the implementation of the human rights in India have to be properly effectuated and implemented the reality of violation of human rights has to be faced with a much more of sincerely and honesty towards the other people of India. Otherwise what is engraved in the constitution in the chapters thereon fundamental rights and directive principles will always remain a distant dream to achieve.

Prof. P. Prasad in his paper on *"Right to Development and Globalisation-Paradigm"* stressed the need for the reduction of poverty in the long run with the acceleration of economic growth and creating employment opportunities by increasing the capabilities of individuals by building peoples participation, involvement and commitment in promoting and sustaining the developmental programme. The new global market must work in his direction to realise right of development to all people as reality.

Saji Thomas in his paper on *"Globalisation and its impact on Human Rights in India"*, highlighted that the term globalisation is to describe the private flow across the world by transitional corporations. It is the integration of world market for goods, services and accumulation of profits for the richest few. He rightly said the state has to play a more responsible role along with well meaning voluntary associations. A powerful global alliance of workers/trade unions, voluntary organisations can do much in countering the onslaught of globalisation and working towards an alternate social order which is a little more just and equitable. Structural Adjustment Programme has brought about adverse impact and effects of globalisation can be countered only by strengthening human rights norms and institutions which protect entitlements such as right to work, right to food, right to education, right to health, right to environment, etc. The human rights movements can strengthen the struggle for human rights and just economic order.

Dr. K. Sreenivasa Rao and Mr. A. Srinivas in their paper entitled *"Globalisation, social justice with reference to right to health of women"*, emphasised that structural adjustment affects vulnerable groups especially women, children, disadvantaged in the form of shock therapy of drastic cut in the welfare provisions. The right to health of women especially rural women are affected by structural adjustment programmes. Right to health for all remained only in paper and not in practice.

Smit. P.B. Pankaja in her paper on *"Structural Adjustment—Role of MNCs"*, has remarked that globalisation has become a subject of very serious discussion in the national economic policies. She has dealt with the meaning of the concepts such SAP, MNC and growth of MNC and also highlighted the role MNCs in India. She also said that it is wrong to assume that the success of MNCs is guaranteed in developed countries and that the domestic firms will not withstand the competition from them. Such apprehensions can be mitigated if sufficient safeguards are taken by the developing nations to regulate the MNCs in home countries and strengthen the home industries.

R. Narayana in his paper on *"Globalisation reflects and affects rights of the child in India"*, remarked that the new economic policy and legal reforms totally negate the implementation of programmes under Article 38 and 39. As a result of SAP the grand vision embodied in the preamble with regard to social and economic justice is slowly vanishing. The rights of the child are affected and neglected under the new region of LPG.

Mr. R.D. Vijayasekhar in his paper on *"Human Rights and Social Justice"*, rightly remarked that the constitutional vision of social justice is seriously affected under the influence of imperial needs. The SAP has no space whatsoever for democratic values of social justice for vulnerable sections. The SAP in setting formidable tasks defending democracy, protecting national sovereignty and ensuring social justice.

Mr. I. Subramanyam in his paper on '*Empowerment of Agricultural Rural Women Labourers and Human Rights in the Context of Globalisation*", stressed that agricultural labourers, who constitute nearly 70 per cent of the total rural labour households, suffer from seasonal unemployment, job insecurity, poverty, indebtedness, bondage, migration, inability to get statutory minimum wages and all sorts of discrimination. Globalisation has affected the right to work of the women agricultural workers.

Dr. (Mrs) M. Vanamala in her paper entitled "*Capital Centric Development Patriarch chain of—Capital, State and Households—The Question of Unfreedoms*", stressed that women in general suffer different forms of disadvantages (unfreedoms) and threats to basic human rights in the socio-economic and household spheres. These unfreedoms reinforce each other. The state, the capital and the household contribute to these unfreedoms at their own levels. These trends form a chain in a market/capital centric/patriarchal transitional society like India. The unfreedoms are getting intensified. Therefore, the protection of human rights in general and that of female rights in particular need a critical evaluation.

Prof. G. Saibaba &
Dr. K. Sreenivasa Rao

List of Contributors

Prof. P. Murali, *Vice-Chancellor, S. V. University.*

Justice Shri. Styabrata Sinha, *Former Chief Justice, High Court* of Andhra Pradesh, Hyderabad.

Justice P. S. Narayana, *Judge, High Court of Andhra Pradesh, Plot No. 4, S.B.I. Officers Colony Moosarambagh, Hyderabad–36.*

Prof. A.S. Seetharamu, *Professor and Head Education Unite, Institute for Social and Economic Change, Nagarabhavi, Bangalore–560 072.*

Prof. D.N. Reddy, *Professor of Economics, University of Hyderabad, Hyderabad.*

Prof. E. Vijayakumar, *Faculty of Law Dean, S.K. University, Anantapur.*

Prof. A. Lakshminath, *Registrar, Nalsar, 3-4-761, Barkatpura, Hyderabad–500 027.*

Prof. D. Venkateswarlu, *Head, Department of Sociology S.V. University, Tirupati.*

Prof. G. Saibaba, Dean, *SSBS and Head and Coordinator, Dept. of Human Rights and Social Development, S.V. University, Tirupati.*

Dr. K. Uma Devi, *Head, Department of Law, Sri Padmavathi Mahila Viswa Vidyalayam, Tirupati.*

Mr. G. Vijay, *Research Scientist, Institute of Social Sciences 6/3/252, Shilpa Apartment, Erramanzil, Hyderabad.*

Mrs. N. Rajeswari, *Teaching Assistant, Department of Human Rights and Social Development, S.V. University, Tirupati.*

Prof. V. Hamalatha Devi, *Professor and Head, Dean Faculty of Law, P.G. Department of Law, S.V. University, Tirupati.*

Prof. P.V. Ramamurti, *Professor of Psychology (Rtd) S.V. University, Tirupati.*

Prof. S. Seshaiah, *Department of Law, Sri Krishnadevaraya University Anantapur.*

Prof. Ranbir Singh, *Director, Nalsar, Hyderabad.*

Prof. P. Prasad, *Head, Department of Economics, S.V. University, University, Tirupati.*

Saji Thomas, *Vigil India Movement, 61, Charles Compbell Road, Cox Town, Bangalore–5600005.*

Dr. K. Sreenivasa Rao, *Assistant Professor, Dept. of Human Rights and Social Development, S.V. University, Tirupati.*

Mr. A. Srinivasu, *Research Scholar, Dept. of Psychology, S.V. University, Tirupati.*

Smt. P. B. Pankaja, *Guest Faculty, Dept. of Human Rights and Social Development, S.V. University, Tirupati.*

Sri. R. Narayana, *Guest Faculty, Dept. of Human Rights and Social Development, S. V. University, Tirupati.*

Mr. R.D. Vijayasekhar, *Guest, Faculty, Dept. of Human Rights and Social Development, S.V. University, Tirupati.*

Mr. I. Subramanyam, *Teaching Assistant, Dept. of Human Rights and Social Development, S.V. University, Tirupati.*

Dr. M. Vanamala, *Reader in Economics, Government Degree College for Women Begumpet, Hyderabad.*

STRUCTURAL ADJUSTMENT AND HUMAN RIGHTS

1

Human Rights:
New Challenges in 2001

Justice Satyabrata Sinha

"The path of Human Rights' does not run smooth and straight. Every day we stumble against the irrational, reason is pushed to one side and rights are trodden underfoot. Many are the words that oppose Human Rights, authoritation regimes, heavy-handed and all-inclusive governmental structures, as well as private groups (think of terrorists organisations) that treat defencies and innocent people with ruthless violence. All those who belong to such authoritarian structures or violent private groups refuse to allow anyone to question or threaten their aggressive impulses and lust of power".

Antonia Cassese.

Introduction

Human being like all other forms of life is part of the nature. Every form of life in its most-minutest form 'cell' gets synthesised and adopts to sustain itself and perishes in a natural way. Necessarily, therefore, human beings follow the same pattern from the beginning to end of life. During the period from birth to death, a human being as a social animal acquries claims and liberties. These claims, liberties, powers and immunities are described under the homonym 'rights". These rights do not owe their existence to any law.

They are gifts of nature. Thomas Jefferson declared that all men are created equally and they are endowed with certain inalienable rights to life, liberty and pursuit of happiness. These rights of man and woman compendiously came to be accepted as 'human Rights'. These are 'irreducible minima' which belong to every member of human race when pitted against the State or other public authorities or group, gangs and other oppressive communities.[2] They are invaluable and cannot be legitimately denied or abrogated by any power of the State.

The movement for 'Human Rights' is part of human history and it is never a lone sojourner. Every time, there is disquieting tendency in the history leading colossal catastrophe, the aftermath necessarily insighted eruption and escalation of thoughts, directed towards 'Human Rights'. In 1188 AD, the Federal Assembly of Kingdom of Leon received from King Alfonsa IX the confirmation of series of rights. King Andrew II of Hungary guaranteed rights against arbitrary arrest and most famous and influential beginning in the saga of 'Human Rights'—Magnacarta was accepted by King John in 1215 AD after a struggle. The French Declaration of the 'Human Rights' of Man and Citizen, 1789 which is an invaluable contribution in the Global Struggle for 'Human Rights', Covenant of League of Nations, 1919, Universal Declaration of Human Rights (UDHR), 1948 and its related charters were added to Human Rights jurisprudence only after tremendous struggle. The history of 'Human Rights' movement is also a history of the challenges faced by it. It also scripted with prognosis for the ailment which we suffer i.e. 'Human Rights' violations.

Constitution of India and Human Rights

It is not possible to define 'Human Rights' in an objective manner. The Universal Declaration of Human Rights, 1948, enumerated at least 27 such broad rights, which are necessary for the establishment of social and international order in which the rights and freedoms can be realised. Parts III and IV of the Constitution of India contain number of rights which are guaranteed 'Human Rights'. Some of these rights are akin to the rights enumerated in other international treaties and chapters.

Protection of Human Rights Act, 1993 defines 'human Rights' as to mean the rights relating to life, liberty, equality and dignity of the individual guaranteed by the Constitution or embodied in international Covenants on Civil and Political Rights (ICCPR) and International Covenant on Economic, Social and Cultural Rights (ICESCR) which were adopted by the General Assembly of United Nations on 16.12.1966. This Act was made by the Parliament "having regard to the changing social realities concern in India and brought about issues relating to 'Human Rights' with a view to bring about greater accountability and transparency in enforcement of laws of the nation." In India, the Movement of Human Rights is a part of social justice which is a conceived and perceived Constitutional goal intended to be practised with all sincerity by the three wings of the State: Legislature, Executive and Judiciary.

The Hon'ble Chief Justice of India—Dr. A.S. Anand while delivering the inaugural Address in the National Seminar of Human Rights conducted by the Department of Law, University of Bombay[3] observed:

> "Thus, social justice is the basis of the progress stability of society and the right to life and liberty as explained and expanded under Article 21 of the Constitution of India, is a part of social justice. Social justice to be meaningful and purposeful must be rooted in the acceptance of human dignity of every man. Social order would violently fall unless full regard is given to human dignity and the failure of social order would... The future of the democracy would be at peril. Therefore let all *human beings unite and walk hand-in-hand to preserve Human dignity.'*

In Indian Context, all penumbral rights relating to life, liberty and dignity (Articles 17, 20, 21, 22, 23, 21, 38(2), 39(3), 42, 43 and 51(A)(3)) and right to equality (Articles 14, 15 and 16, 38(1), 39(1), 39(a), (b) etc.) are 'Human Rights', some of which are concerned with life and some other with liberty. Indeed, in A.P. Pollution Control Board vs. Prof. M.V. Naidu[4], the Supreme Court observed that Human Rights aspects concern liberty. Keeping this in view, we may deliberate upon albeit in brief-the status and challenges of 'Human Rights' to life, liberty, equality and dignity *Chief and Human Rights.*

Child and Human Rights

The child is a person within the legal meaning. All the rights, claims liberties, which inhere a human being, also belong to the child. Greed, helplessness, poverty and exploitation, however, are inimically dispossessed of to the child. Ignorance, tenderness made a child gullible to adults' evil design. In times of war and peace it is the child who suffers more than the elder. Despite U.D.H.R. and other such international efforts billions of children were denied human rights. Ultimately in 1989 the General Assembly of U.N.O. in the convention on rights of the child (CRC) adopted the rights drafted by UN Commission on human rights. It is a set of international standards and measures intended to protect and promote the well being of the children in the society. The Charter is guided by the principle *'first call for children'*—a principle that the essential needs of the children should be given highest priority in allocation of resources at all times. It obligates signatory States to respect and ensure that children get a fair and equitable deal in society. The Charter contains 41 Articles and recognises the right of the child to live with dignity, right to health, nutritious food and right to beauty of childhood.

The society and other groups have thus far denied the right of the child to education and decent life. The child was economically exploited by forcibly engaging as commercial, farm, domestic and industrial servants and was treated as a slave with or without connivance of the parents. A large body of Legislations like Apprentices Act 1961, The Children (Pledging of Labour) Act 1933, The Child Labour (Prevention and Regulation) Act 1986, The Bonded Labour System (Abolition) Act 1976, Motor Transport Workers Act, 1961, Factories Act 1948, The Minimum Wages Act, 1948. The Plantations Labour Act 1951, The Trade unions Act, 1926, The Workmen's Compensation Act 1923, The Mines Act 1952, Beedi and Cigar Workers (Conditions of Employment) Act 1966 and Merchant Shipping Act 1958 either abolish or regulate child labour.

The Supreme Court of India in a large number of cases has strenuously come down against the executive and against those who exploit children, and issued appropriate directions. In Unni Krishnan vs. State of A.P.[5], the Supreme Court held that it is the fundamental right of every child to have education up to the age of fourteen years. The decision in Unnikrishnan's case lead to far-reaching directions given by the Supreme Court in M.C. Mehta vs. State of Tamil Nadu[5] where the Supreme Court in its activist role directed every State Government to deposit an amount of Rs. 25,000/- as detrained expenses of the child if it is to be compulsorily weaned from economic activity and send to education. Anganwadi and Balwadi Schemes and Integrated Child Development Programmes aim at good health and nutrition to the children.

Notwithstanding the State efforts, legislatively as well as executively, social evil of child abuse continues. This is the perennial challenge to the human rights movement. Whether the legislation is insufficient or whether implementation is inadequate are the two questions to which all of us have to address ourselves. In majority of African Nations, South American Nations as well as Indian subcontinent still billions of children suffer from poverty, ill-health and exploitation. A concerted unified effort on the part of everyone is more than desired.

In so far as the judiciary is concerned, we have accepted principle that our fundamental rights chapter is required to be interpreted compatibly in accordance with international law[7]. An interesting question is whether violation of International Treaty Law gives rise to legitimate expectation to a parent of the child. Such a question has come up in High Court of Australia in Minister for immigration and Ethnic Affairs vs. Teoh[8]. In the said case when the Minister passed an order of deportation of a citizen of Hongkong, who was staying in Australia without valid permit the same was challenged as violation of the U.N. Covenant on rights of the child as deportation of parent would deprive him the job which would deprive the child of right to good food and health. Though the Chapter was not incorporated in Australian Law, the Australian High Court ruled that nevertheless it gives rise to legitimate expectation that the decision maker would comply with International Charter.

Women and Human Rights

As per the U.N. Report, 1980 women constitute fifty percent of world's population. They perform two-third of work hours, but receive one-tenth of world's income and own one-hundredth percent of world's property. They constitute more than half of Indian population. They are denied life, liberty and dignity. The right to equality before law is available only to a fortunate few. They suffer discrimination and their self-sacrifice or self-denial further add to the problem. Vienna declaration on Elimination of All forms of Discrimination against Women (CEDAW), 1979 ratified by UNO on 18.12.1979 takes note of the discrimination against women and mandates of all member States to take all appropriate measures including legislation to modify or abolish gender based discrimination in the existing laws, regulations, customs and practice. All forms of discrimination on ground of gender is violative of fundamental freedoms and human rights. The General Assembly of U.N.O. on 4.12.1986 adopted resolution on Right to Development recognising the right of every woman to develop. The escalating emergence of women's rights is not an accidental or sporadic occurrence. The Constitution of India prohibits discrimination only on the basis of sex. Further, it empowers the State to take all necessary steps for the upliftment of women. In Government of A.P. vs. P.B. Vijay Kumar[9] for the first time the Supreme Court laid down that Article 15(3) can be read into Article 16 to sustain any special provision favouring women. The reasoning is as follows.

"....The ambit of Article 16(2) is more limited in scope than Article 15(1) because it is confined to employment of office under the State. Article 15(1), on the other hand, covers the entire range of State activities...Since Article 16 does not touch upon any special provision for women being made by the State. It cannot in any manner derogate from the power conferred upon the State in this connection under Article 15(3). This power conferred by Article 15(3) is wide enough to cover the entire range of State activity including employment under the State... To say that under Article 15(3), job opportunities for women cannot be created would be to cut at the very root of the underlying inspiration behind this Article. Making special provisions for women in respect of employment or posts under the State is an integral part of Article 15(3). This conferred under Article 15(3) is not whittled down in any manner by Article 16.

The concept of equality vis-a-vis women does not mean that the State is denied the right to provide preferential treatment for women in all State activity. In Muthamma vs. Union of India,[10] Air India vs. Nargesh Mirja[11], the Supreme Court struck down discriminatory service conditions requiring female employees to obtain government permission before marriage and denying married and pregnant women the right to be employed. By displaying activist role in Visakha vs. State of Rajasthan[12], (noticing the legislative and executive vacuum to prevent sexual harassment at the workplace), the Supreme Court relying on the provisions in the Beijing Statement of Principles of the Independence of the Judiciary, 1995, CEDAW, 1979, and the Protection of Human Rights Act, 1993 held that women have right to gender equality to work with dignity and to a working environment available and protected from sexual harassment or abuse. It was categorically held that every incident of sexual harassment at the work place results in violation of fundamental right of gender equality and the right to life and liberty. The same view was reiterated in Appeal Export Promotion Council vs. A.K. Chopra[13] and it was further held that sexual harassment is misconduct in service law making the delinquent person liable for dismissal.

The employment statistics show that in agricultural sector which I call 'earth collar' jobs, seventy per cent of the labour is women. The dominant classes in the rural areas seldom treat these agricultural labour as human beings and at slightest opportunity they exploit them sexually. In payment of wages and supply of food etc. the women are discriminated. In blue collar and white collar employment sectors there is increasing presence of women as employees at all levels. The insult verbally or by sign language in tolerated by women in silence for the fear of losing respect in the society. All the cases of harassment are not reported. Visakha and Apparel Corporation cases have no doubt part of the Indian law. But still women continue to suffer insult at the work place which is again a perennial challenge to the human rights activists.

Prisoners and Human Rights

The old exploiting the young; the man exploiting the woman; the rich exploiting the poor; and the antisocial exploiting citizen are all aspects of open society. There is another society behind the prison walls where large number of human beings are denied human rights. Legal justice requires that offenders of law should be brought to book and punished. Within this Constitutionally accepted practice of protecting the society from abnormal human beings, at the stage of investigation as suspects; at the stage of trial as under-trials; and at the stage of punishment as incarcerated human beings citizens are denied the rights. Though human approach to reformation of the prisoners is very much part of the social science of criminology, there is much to be done in this field. In the prechncts of jail what happens is known to the jail administrator. For fear of facing torture, the 'principle of silence' is rule and does not allow the violators to come to the fore. Under-trial prisoners are denied the right to speedy trial which is a human right. The prisoners are denied the rights of human beings. The Supreme Court of India in a caterna of decisions has recognised this. The Andhra pradesh High Court has noticed all these judgments and in Mir Mohammed Ali vs. Government of Andhra Pradesh[14] has given number of directions for releasing of under-trial prisoners who have been languishing in prison without proper trial for a long time. In all societies there is a need to sensitise civilised world to the reality that the accused and prisoners have rights, which are almost equal to the rights of those people in the society.

HIV-AIDS and Human Rights

Caught in the coils of HIV-AIDS, humankind is struggling to extricate itself from the recent scourge of the 20th century.[15] The recent State-wide statistics of number of such patients shows the situation is alarming. The problem throws up lot of challenges to the Human Rights Law. The Indian Legal system is not fully geared up to face the challenges. There is lot of legislative vacuum in the field. Whether HIV AIDS disease can be treated as a problem of public health bringing under the Epidemic Diseases Act, 1897 and Public Health Act? Whether sex workers who are imprisoned under Immoral Traffic (Prevention) Act, 1956 can be denied right to life by denying the release after period of sentence on the ground that they require treatment for HIV-AIDS? Whether the doctor treating the patient is under obligation to reveal to the society about the disease without violating hippocractic oath? Whether the State and society can deny fundamental rights and human rights to HIV-AIDS patients. These are some of the challenges we should be prepared to face.

In Lucy D'Souza vs. State of Goa[6], the Bombay High Court considered the question whether a citizen suffering from AIDS can be isolated from the others. It was held:

> "isolation, undoubtedly, has several serious consequences. It is an invasion upon the liberty of a person. It can affect a person very adversely in many matters including economic. It can also lead to social ostracisation. But in matters like this individual rights has to be balanced the in public interest. In fact liberty of an individual and public health are not opposed to each other but are well in accord. Even if there is a conflict between the right of an individual and public interest, the former must yield to the latter. That apart, isolation is not merely in the interest of the society. In a given case, it may also be in the interest of an AIDS patient, because the may become desperate and lose all hopes of survival and therefore, has to be saved against himself. Perhaps, bearing in mind all these factors, the experts have considered isolation as one of the preventive measures."

On the above premises, Section 53(1)(viii) of the Goa, Daman and Diu Public Health act, 1985 which empowered the Health Officer to isolate a person who is found to be a positive for Acquired Immuno Deficiency Syndrome (AIDS), was upheld.

In P.N. Swamy, vs. Station House officer[17], a Division Bench of Andhra Pradesh High Court directed that women rescued from brothel houses who were found to be infected with HIV, be taken to welfare houses to make them learn vocational courses. It was also directed to separate the children of these women to be sent to welfare hostel having regard to the rights of the children. The Court recognised the fundamental right to life and liberty of even those who suffer from HIV-AIDS.

In Mr. 'X' vs. Hospital 'Z'[8], the Supreme Court considered the right of a person infected with HIV-AIDS from jurisprudential point of view vis-a-vis Article 21 of the Constitution and held that where there is a clash of two fundamental rights between right to privacy as in the case of AIDS patient and the fundamental right to lead a healthy life of another person, the right which would advance the public morality or public interest, would alone be enforced through the process of Court. In the said case, Mr. X decided to marry one Ms. Y. But the marriage was called off because after conducting blood test, Hospital Z found Mr. X to be HIV-positive. A case was filed for damages before the National Consumer Redressal Commission against the Hospital on the ground that the Hospital violated the right to privacy by disclosing the confidential information as to HIV positive. The National Commission dismissed the application. Before the Supreme Court, it was contended that the Hospital violated hypocractic oath to maintain the confidentiality about the disease of the patient and as they violated, they are liable in damages to Mr. X. The Supreme Court held that as proposed marriage with Ms. Y. carried with it the health risk to an identifiable person to be protected from being infected with the communicable disease from Mr. X, the right to confidentiality was not enforceable. It was also argued before the Supreme Court that the right to privacy under Article 21 of the Constitution has been infringed by the Hospital.

The argument was repealed by the Supreme Court as under:

> "The contention of the learned counsel that every young man or, for that matter, a woman, has a right to marry cannot be accepted in the absolute terms in which it is being contended. Having regard to the age and the biological needs, a person may have a right to marry but this right is not without a duty. If that person is suffering from any communicable venereal disease or is impotent so that marriage would be a complete failure or that his wife would seek divorce from him on that ground, that person is under a moral, as also legal duty, to inform the woman with whom the marriage is proposed that he was not physically healthy and that he was suffering from a disease which was likely to be communicated to her. In this situation, the right to marry and duty to inform about his ailment are vested. In the same person... ... Such a right for these reasons also, would be an exception to the general rule that every 'Right' has a correlative "Duty".

Therefore, the right to marry in the case of a person suffering with AIDS is given restrictive meaning as held by the Supreme Court in the following terms:

> "AIDS" is the product of indisciplined sexual impulse. This impulse, being the notorious human falling if not disciplined, can afflict and overtake anyone how high so ever of, for that matter, how low he may be in the social strata. The patients suffering from the dreadful disease "AIDS" deserve full sympathy. They are entitled to all respects as human beings. Their society cannot, and should not, be avoided, which otherwise, would have had psychological impact upon them. They have to have their avocation. Government jobs of service cannot be denied to them.... But, "sex" with them or possibility thereof has to be avoided as otherwise they would infect and communicate the dreadful disease to others. The Court cannot assist that person to achieve that object."

There are other problem areas like compelling a suspected AIDS patient to undergo serological tests and separating the children of AIDS patients from their parents.

Refugees and Human Rights

UDHR specially recognises the right to seek and enjoy asylum in an alien country. The cross border exodus of exploited human beigns every where has created new problem area of "stateless citizens". The disturbing trends of religious bigotry and ethnicism has created social tensions sometimes resulting in genocide and large scale migration. In East Asia, Europe, Central Africa, the history during the past decade has thrown challenges to the Human Rights in this area of Human Rights.

International Refuge law seems to revolve around two main pillars—the norm making process at the International level with a strong focus on the evolution of a right regime to protect and provide for refugees and the practical aspects of international and domestic State policies, which are reflected in the actual observance of or modified compliance with, these international norms, or simply put, in the practice of States. The implications of providing asylum have several ramifications on the individual State in its social, political and economic structure. Any such decision must remain the prerogative of the individual state and therefore immigration laws have been the exclusive jurisdiction of the individual State, with minimal international interference. Thus, we have two seemingly irreconcilable perspectives. One provides for the protection and the prevention of violation of human rights, both at the domestic and international level, and the other providing for the importance of State interests and the sovereign power of the State to determine its policies with regard to immigration and asylum rights. The main hurdle in incorporating a strong human rights regime in refugee protection is the failure to point out a clear addressee of the obligations of Human Rights protection. Treaty and customary human rights obligations usually rest clearly with one State, and the relation can be clearly established between Individuals or groups with the Government or the State in question. This domestic framework is open to international concern and coercion, in the form of sanctions by the international community. This framework, however, is lacking, in the context of refugee protection, as no obligations are spelt out vis-a-vis the reguee with respect to the receiving state or any other state of the international community.

The limited obligation of non-refoulement prohibits forcible return to any country where the person concerned is likely to face severe human rights violations. However, the lack of clearly defined legal principles defeat the purposes of the non-refoulement principle by not providing for any comprehensive durable solutions. Also, the failure to read in general human rights obligations of the international community with respect to aliens and especially refugees has resulted in a situation where the obligation to provide for the right to asylum is dictated by the policies of the individual states.

Other Challenges

Activities of followers of political ideology with faith in extremist violence and radicalism have resulted in conditions which are appalling. The people are denied the right to choice as to the residence and avocation. The people who lost limbs due to land mine blasts and those who lost the limbs due to terrorists' amputation heckle at human rights activists who bring the cases of law breakers before Courts complaining human rights violations. The complaint of violation of human rights by the State in the case of those who themselves violate human rights of others is a big challenge in a democratic system. Apart from this, the State sponsored terrorism either in enforcing the municipal law or for enforcing the foreign policy for various reasons assumes a subject of perennial debate. Thus, larger issues are a cause for the convenient gloss over the human rights of those unfortunate people who are physically challenged (handicapped) and mentally challenged (handicapped) for no fault of theirs. Needless to reiterate, Human Rights of those challenged persons are not recognised at all.

Conclusion

The world is caught up in economic liberalisation and global market syndrome. Increasing awareness in the affluent countries for better comforts for their citizens would necessarily result in depriving the human rights in other countries. As we discuss, human rights in this hall, elsewhere the children are denied the right to dignified life and women are subjected to deprivation and insult. The more emphasis on the practice of Human Rights results in equally forceful opposite reaction and there are more and more violations of Human Rights. But there need not be scope for pessimism, for an honest appraisal of Human Rights practices would go a long way for giving effect to international treaty or convention rights as well as Human Rights in the Constitution.

REFERENCES

1. Dias 'Jurisprudence'; 1985; Butterworths, London.
2. Krishna Iyer V.R.: Human Rights in India: Iagore Law Lectures, 2000, Eastern Law House, Calcutta, New Delhi.
3. Human Rights and Law: National and Global Perspectives, Published by Snow White Publishers, 1997.
4. (1999) 2 SCC 718.
5. AIR 1993, SC 2178.
6. AIR 1997 SC 699.
7. *(a)* Jolly George Varghese vs. The Bank of Chochin: AIR 1980 SC 470.
   (b) Rajagopal vs. State of Tamil Nadu: AIR 1995 SC 264.
   (c) D.K. Basu vs. State of West Bengal: AIR 1997 SC 610.

8. [(1995) 69 ALJR 423]
9. AIR 1995 SC1648 (1995) 3 SCC 613.
10. AIR 1979 SC 1968.
11. (1981) 4 SCC 335.
12. (1997) 6 SCC 241.
13. (1999) 1 SCC 759.
14. 2000(4) ALI 541 (DB).
15. Justice M N Rao: "Reflections on Law and Society: 2000-pp 10-19.
16. AIR 1990 BOMBAY 355.
17. 1998 (1) ALD 755 (DB)
18. AIR 1999 SC 495.

2

Impact of Structural Adjustment Policies on the Basic Human Rights of Vulnerable Groups such as Women, Children, Dalits and Tribals

Justice P.S. Narayana

Section2(d) of the Protection of Human Rights Act 1993 defines Human Rights as:

> "In this Act unless the context otherwise requires, human rights means the rights relating to life, liberty, equality and dignity of the individual guaranteed by the Constitution or embodied in the International Covenants and enforceable by Courts in India."

It is needless to point out that the subject of the day is a vast one but because of the time constraint, certain essential aspects alone can be touched.

In National Human Rights Commission vs. State of Arunachal Pradesh (AIR 1996 SC 1234) the observations of the Apex Court may be relevant in this context:

> "Our Constitution confers rights on every human being and certain other rights on citizens. Every person is entitled to equality before law and equal protection of the laws. So also, no person can be deprived of his right of personal liberty

except according to procedure established by law. Thus the State is bound to protect the life and liberty of every human being be he a citizen or otherwise".

The relevant provisions, Legislations, Rules, Covenants etc., may be specified as follows:

Fundamental Rights and Directive principles of State policy

Articles 330 to 342 of the Constitution of India

The protection of Human Rights Act 1993

Protection of Civil Rights Act 1955

National Commission for Women Act 1990

National Commission for Minorities Act 1992

National Commission for Safai Karamcharis Act 1993

National Commission for Backward Classes Act 1993

S.Cs. and S.Ts. (Prevention of Atrocities) Act 1989

Persons with Disabilities (Equal opportunities, Protection of Rights and Full Participation) Act 1995

The National Trust for Welfare of persons with Autism, Cerebral , Palsy, Mental Retardation and Multiple Disabilities Act 1999

The Commission of Sati (Prevention) Act 1987

The Pre-natal Diagnostic Techniques (Regulation and prevention of Mosque) Act 1994

Juvenile Justice Act 1986

The Child Labour (Prohibition and Regulation) Act 1986

The Indecent Representation of Women (Publication) Act 1986

The Medical Termination of Pregnancy Act 1971

The Muslim Women (Protection of Rights on Divorce) Act 1986

The Employment of Manual Scavengers and Construction of Dry Latrines (Prohibition) Act 1993

Rules and also Regulations connected therewith.

Universal Declaration of Human Rights 1948

International Covenant on Civil and Political Rights 1996

International Convention on the elimination of all forms of Racial Discrimination 1966

The list is only illustrative and not exhaustive

The historical background of Human Rights can be traced even from Vedic times, Babylonian Laws, Magna Cartas, Virginia Bill of Rights, French Declaration of the Rights of Man and during the World wars too several Nations suffered serious set backs and human sufferings and miseries taught the humanity of the World the importance of basic Human Rights and the concept of Human Rights became more an International phenomenon, well governed by not only Municipal law but also several declarations, treaties and covenants which has been referred to supra. Several of the statutory provisions and the subordinate legislations relating thereto mentioned above, deal with these aspects only.

India is a multi-linguistic, multi-cultural and multi-religious State, a sub-continent, which is declared to be "secular". Though often the uniform Civil Code is voiced, the tone is feeble due to the various pressure groups and political considerations as well. Neither Shah Bano Begum's case nor the Muslim Women (Protection of Rights on Divorce) Act 1986 made the Muslim section to think over about the same, nor the traditional Hindu Society is serious of the uniformity inspite of the set-back of having ancient Hindu law codified by different controversial legislations. Be that Christian or Parsi society, the fate appears to the same. Though religion has to be separated from State, it being a faith of a particular person, the growing alarming religious loyalty at the cost of the Nation's interest is really blameworthy. I am not interested in discussing this aspect any further for the reason that it will be out of context.

Sections 376-A, 376-B, 376-C, 376-D, 3-04-B, 498-A in I.P.C., Sections 113-A and 113-B in Indian Evidence Act are all provisions introduced keeping in view the growing atrocities and crimes against women. Because of the personal laws, the rights of women in the country also are not uniform. Despite the same, several legislations dealing with rights of women are uniform. Dowry harassments, dowry deaths, sex crimes, matrimonial disputes, maintenance claims, may be certain areas which can be mentioned in relation to women vis-a-vis Human Rights. At the World Conference on Women in 1985, Kay Fraleign stated:

> "Human rights issues are so interwoven that no advance can be made in one area without reference to another. Perhaps the most important is the need to strengthen the perception that all human rights are linked to the protection of women rights".

Warren Christopher at World Conference on Human rights in 1993 said:

> "Violence and discrimination against women don't just victimise individuals, they hold back whole sections by confining the human potential of half the population. Guaranteeing human rights is a moral imperative with respect to both women and men. It is also an investment in making whole Nations stronger, fairer and better."

In Visakha vs. State of Rajasthan (AIR 1997 SC 3011), the Apex Court had dealt with enforcement of basic human rights in the context of sexual harassment at work places, *See also* AIR 1999 SC 625. Decided cases are numerous where Courts had granted appropriate reliefs to women by issuing directions at the instance of aggrieved parties of organisations for enforcement of fundamental rights and other legal rights too. There is also criticism that Courts are more sympathetic towards this class and they got the relief even in totally undeserving cases at times. This cannot be accepted as true for the reason that at times while exercising discretion Courts may err also and those are only bonafide errors. There is no doubt serious criticism from certain quarters that the provisions relating to dowry or women harassment are being more misused to implicate the innocent in a mood of anger and only to wreck vengeance. Human Rights and Gender equality also may be relevant in this context. *See* SIR 1997 SC 2366, AIR 1951 SC 2267, AIR 1992 SCW 3682.

Policy of Juvenile Reformatory Institutions and Human Rights is another facet of the present day topic. There are certain legislations like Juvenile Justice Act 1986 replacing Children's Act. Several of the provisions of different Labour Legislations also deal with the welfare and protection of children. In Sheela Barse's case (AIR 1987 Sc 656) the Apex Court in the case of observation home observed that the society has to follow not only statutory requirements but also Constitutional provisions. Child prostitution is another area where Human Rights of children are at jeopardy. AIR 1997 SC 3021—Guarav Jain vs. Union of India. See AIR 1995 SCW 4100. In Vishal Jeet vs. Union of India (AIR 1990 SC 1412), suitable directions to take necessary measures to eradicate child prostitution, were issued. Child exploitation also is very relevant. 1997(1) Ker LT 130, AIR 1997 SC 3021, AIR 1997 Bom 349, AIR 1997 Raj 250, (1989) 3 SCC 1, AIR 1998 SC 236.

Structural adjustment policies of Government may be more relevant in the context of their impact on the groups of society. The most affected group of this country will be the Scheduled Castes and Scheduled Tribes, the downtrodden masses of this country. There are the oppressed and unfortunate sections of Indian society from time immemorial. It is no doubt true that even from the advent of Indian Constitution, several benefits were conferred on these sections and though because of these policies, there is some improvement, it cannot be said to be remarkable or outstanding. In that view of the matter, the beneficial measures though unproductive in nature are welfare measures and hence Courts should be slow in disturbing these benefits conferred on these classes either by way of reservations, scholarships, facilities subsidies and other like benefits. It is this province where because of recent policies, these groups are affected. Several of the penal legislations like Protection of Civil Rights Act, SCs and STs. (Prevention of Atrocities) Act had not brought about notable changes in the society though these may deter the public to some extent. It is the real social change which is essential and social reformation alone will be the suitable answer and not Legislations on paper. I may be very critical but it is a fact that several legislations are more on paper and not being practical in being implemented because of social non-cooperation. Structural adjustment policies vis-a-vis Human Rights and real change in the society to take into the fold of the main stream, the segments of SCs and STs are closely interlinked being Government pursuing economic policies, social policies, in substance political decisions only. In C.A. Rajendran vs. Union of India (AIR 1968 SC 507) it was held that Article 16(4) of the Constitution does not confer any right on the petitioner and there is no Constitutional obligation imposed on the Government to make such reservation and Article 16(4) is an enabling provision and confers a discretionary power on the State to make a reservation either at the stage of initial recruitment or at the stage of promotion in favour of backward class citizens, which in its opinion is not adequately represented in the services of the State. In Post Graduate Institute of Medical Education and Research, Chandigarh vs. Faculty Association and others (1998) 4 SCC 1) it was held that the special provision under Article 16(4) of the Constitution must strike a balance between relevant considerations and proceed objectively and it has been indicated in Indra Sahawny's case that Article 16(4) is not in the nature of exception to Articles 16(1) and 16(2), but an instance of classification permitted by Article 16(1). In State of Tripura vs. Namia Majumdar (1998) 9 SCC 217, it was held that a female or a forward caste marrying a person of Scheduled Caste will not be entitled to reservation under Article 16 of the

Constitution. Reservations relating to these classes of Society had been well dealt with in AIR 1997 Bom 1, AIR 1999 SC 791, AIR 1993 SC 477, AIR 1976 SC 490, AIR 1976 SC 2381, AIR 1985 SC 1495, AIR 1964 SC 1823, AIR 1971 SC 1777, AIR 1991 SC 2288, 2001(8) SCC 664, 2001(2) SCC 538. These groups constitute a sizeable percentage through out the country. Irrespective of any Government being in power, no Government is taking away the benefits conferred on these groups but while pursuing the policies the nonproductive so-called welfare measures are being curtailed on the ground that it is for the economic progress of the country. It is no doubt true that the economists do express the opinion that populist measures or vote catching devices adopted by political parties by introducing unproductive schemes or benefits, are not in National interest. Nation means "people" and these groups also are "people" who definitely need a helping hand. Attempts are being made to eradicate untouchability, to permit entry into temples with the approval of Society. We often come across resistance from other groups of the Society. When these sections assert their rights both political and social as well, there are several reported instances in this country which had resulted in unruly violence and blood-shed. This is more a delicate social problem and the reformists of the Society should shoulder this responsibility to solve such problems in the best interest of this Holy Bharat. The problems of the minorities also at times are as alarming as that of the other groups of Society. These are all diversified problems which this country is facing but however there is unity even in such diversity. Nationalism is more an emotional feeling. Patriotism is the price which a citizen can definitely possess, assert in deep devotion towards the mother land. I am conscious of the fact that these words of mine are deviation from the topic of the day. However, inasmuch as the general subject relating to policies is the subject of the day, these words cannot be said to be totally irrelevant. The recent decision of the Central Government to amend the Industrial Disputes

Act 1947 and Labour Laws permitting lay-off, retrenchment, and closure of industrial units had been hailed by the Industrialists as a developmental step and the liberalised policy to promote the expansion of this sector as a well thought policy but however the same is criticised by certain quarters as an attack on workers rights. This is a field where definitely a balance has to be maintained keeping in view the industrial growth and also workers right especially in the light of the social conditions prevailing in this country.

Our country is a welfare State. It is no doubt true that Socialistic pattern of society and the concept of mixed economy had proved to be not well advised policies as far as Indian economy is concerned, especially in the light of the proved data of heavy losses and closure of certain units and taking over of certain units by private sector. Though the concept of police State disappeared long back, in the light of the International compulsions the recent shift appears to be more on the side of private sector. The Information Technology and Cyber Law have gained tremendous popularity which is considered to be a step towards modernisation and globalisation.

I have no manner of doubt in my mind that the structural adjustment and policies followed from nineties do have far reaching consequences on the human rights of vulnerable groups. Privatisation of public sector at a remarkable rapid speed had resulted in unemployment growth. Ours is a country of man-power and under the guise of modernisation and progress if the entrepreneurs and Industrialists engage the techniques to reduce the utilisation of man power to the maximum possible, the suffering class will be the poorer sections of the Society. The reduction of subsidy to poor, vulnerable sections of the Society in the recent times also cannot be said to be a measure in the interest of the Society. Development and progress always must be viewed with care and caution and should not be at the peril of helpless and downtrodden.

Some may say that these measures are unproductive but such measures are obligatory on the part of a welfare State. The prices of the essential commodities also had gone up to a considerable extent because of the sharp raise in procurement prices of food grains. It is needless to state the devaluation of currency also is an essential factor which had the impact of sharp price raise of essential commodities. While formulating policies in a welfare State like India, no doubt progress should be taken as paramount consideration but should not be at the total deprivation of ordinary human rights of vulnerable sections of the Society and maintenance of balance in this regard is essential.

3

Structural Adjustment Policy and Human Rights-A Philosophical Analysis

A.S. Seetharamu

The New Deal

A new economic policy was adopted in India in 1991. This policy shift embraced several dimensions of India's national life. The goal was to move away steadily from an agricultural economy towards an industrial economy. Liberalisation of controls on trade, investments and capital markets, privatisation of production of goods and supply of services, disinterments in the public sector, squeezing of the State machinery for governance, promoting global competitiveness for India's agriculture, industry, trade and services, market determination of production, distribution and pricing of goods and services, decentralisation of development planning and governance, an orientation towards a regime of patents, modernisation of information services, communication networks and management structures, a shift from public subsidies towards 'users pay' principles, and similar measures are illustrative strategies of the policy shift.

Need for a new Deal

Where was the need for this shift in economic policy?

Nearly 40 years of planning for change and development in India was heading towards a shipwreck by the year 1990. Escalating poverty (estimated at 37 per cent of the then population of 800 million persons, sprawling inflation [in double digit figures], rising unemployment, burgeoning population, sluggish growth rates, crisis in balance of payments situation, abysmally low performance in global volume of trade, shark-fashioned consumption of public expenditures by non-plan heads, unbearable dead-wood in government administrative machinery and public sector undertaking, State Corporations in the 'red' in regard to performance and profits, never-ending scenarios in regard to illiteracy, morbidity, infant, child and maternal mortality situation, eluding goals of universalisation of primary education, health, housing, sanitation, water supply and rural electrification, problems of infrastructure and markets, continuation of social tensions and conflicts rooted in caste and class based inequalities, political unrest and regionalism, and like this a variety of issues and concerns led to a generally shared feeling of a failure of the 'State' in India. The State in India had been highly centralised in its control over the economy and in its own development initiatives. In sum, the economy had been trapped in a low equilibrium stalemate. It needed a metamorphic resuscitation. Helping hands were stretched by international financial institutions like the IMF and the World Bank on conditions that the State in India would subject itself to metamorphic policy changes and intensive strategic treatments that have been paraphrased in the earlier section under the 'New Deal'.

Criticism of the New Deal

The response of the India State for expectations from international donor agencies has been quick, positive, vibrant and overwhelming. Over the years the State also exercised caution and circumspection in overseeing a smooth passage to the reforms process. It responded to widespread criticism that social sector is being ignored in planning and investment measures. A National Reneval Fund has been set up to finance education, health, forestry, water and sanitation projects, rural housing, employment, women's development and similar concerns. This way it has tried to create a Social Safety Net. Several projects in these sectors are also being supported on a loan-cum-grant basis. All these measures have been taken to justify the reform process. The whole process is described as Structural Adjustment Policy. Inspite of assurances by the State that the reforms are pro-growth, pro-poor and pro-national interests there have been criticisms that the reforms are detrimental to the realisation of basic human rights in India. While the government, the bureaucracy and the pro-reform lobby flag the TINA card (There Is No Alternative), the critics maintain that the new deal is a sell out of human rights and human freedoms by the established vested interest groups in the country. There is a convergence of interests across business, commerce, industry, trade and services (add 'big' as an adjective everywhere), political leadership, bureaucracy and global partners for the same. The proverbial 'common man' is uninformed, helpless and despondent against this imposing establishment. Some of the illustrations in recent years of organised attack are; (a) imposition of a 'social clause' and of sanctions on trade with India in regard to tobacco products and carpets by the World Trade Organisation as the production sector for these goods employs child labour (b) patenting of traditional medicines of India which use neem and turmeric by some crafty Indian-born American scientists. Both these strategies were aborted by human rights activists and vigilant Indian public. (c) In the guise of popularisation of bio-technology, a large number and variety of indigenous, genetic seeds are systematically being marginalised. But Cotton is a recent example. Labour-intensive agricultural technology is being mechanised. In the process, large scale unemployment and underemployment is observed in the agricultural sector. Like this, there have been criticisms on several grounds of the New Deal, the economic reforms process in India.

Crux of the Debate

Reality of life in India is that there has been an onset of metamorphic changes since 1991. This mega-policy change variously described as economic reforms, structural adjustment policy or new deal has been initiated, sponsored, promoted, fostered, executed, monitored and managed by the State in India. Even the Indian States including West Bengal and Kerala where the reigning political ideology is communism have also welcomed and supported the reform process, although with certain reservations. They have been eager either to woo foreign direct investment or to squeeze public expenditures. What is the "TRUTH' about economic reforms process? Is this reform process in the interest, well-being, freedom and happiness of the 'common man'? Does it promote and catalyse the goals of justice, equality ad welfare of the masses of India? Specifically does the process phenomenally reduce poverty in India and redress class and sceptical imbalances? Or alternatively does it further depress the standard of living, quality of life of the people in this country? Will there be a furtherance of the goals of Constitutional life in India or will it only be a case of forbearance for the helpless, mute, ignorant and suffering millions of the country? Will it make the country affluent without being an affront on human rights and human freedoms? What after all do we mean by human rights? In what ways can it be affected or enriched by economic reforms?

Further, if the reforms process is considered as a fait accompli, then, how can it be regulated, channelised and directed towards a secure, stable and faster realisation of human rights and human freedoms? What are the relative roles of the State, the mass media, the intellectuals and the civil society organisations in ensuring human rights and human freedoms in the thick of the reform process? How can the on-going process develop a human face? What is the knowledge-base required for collective rationality in the exercise of choices within the reforms process for welfare, well-being and happiness of the common people? How can the reform process be mounted on superior and strong ethical foundations? Some of the significant questions flagged herein will be addressed in this paper. The questions are philosophical in nature as they examine the Truths embedded in Reality. The on-going economic reforms is the reality while justice, equality, individual rights and freedoms are the Truths of life and the universe around us. Truth is that which is permanent, which transcends the limitations of time and space. Reality is that which is apparent, visible, within the ambit of human experience. The strategies and interventions of the reform process are reality. Does this reality promote Truth?

Assumptions and their Validity

Is it right to infer that the on-going structural adjustment policy (SAP) is escalating poverty and inequality in India? Was there no poverty and deprivation in the country before 1991? Did poverty get reduced substantially and were basic human rights realised in the post 1951 and pre-1991 era? Is the appalling State of Indian society in the areas of primary health, basic education, literacy, employment, water supply, sanitation, rural roads, electricity etc; due to SAP? One need not struggle to get answers to these questions. Extensive literature on India's development performance has appeared on surface along with the euphoria associated with 50 years of India's independence, 50 years of India's life as Republic and the new millennium. A summary update is presented here as the context for analysis of concerns and issues in regard to SAP and human rights.

The three five years plans of India beginning with the first plan and the three annual plans 1966-1969 assumed that growth will take care of equity. There were no specific strategies for poverty alleviation, employment generation and balanced regional development. It took nearly 20 years (1969-1974, fourth five year plan, to at least get acclimatised to slogans such as 'Food for work', 'Garibi Hatao' and 'Basic Needs' in the planning process. Even at the time of the sixth five year plan (1979 AD), every alternate person in India was identified to be Below Poverty Line (BPL). The BPL ratio came down to 36 per cent by 1993 (ES/GOI/ 1993). The latest NSSO estimates of poverty in India in 2000 AD, based on a large sample survey analysis is 26 per cent. [NSSO, 55th Round]. It is to be noted that while the poor in India in absolute numbers were estimated at 320 million in 1973-74, this number remained the same even by 1993 inspite of the BPL percentage falling from 55 to 37 per cent. However, the poor in absolute numbers has fallen to 260 million by 2000 AD. Falling population growth rates during the 1990s may be one of the significant contributors to this decline.

Another significant variable in human rights analysis is employment. There was no attempt at scientific measurement of unemployment in India till the late sixties of the 20th century. A definition of 'full employment' in terms of standard person years (SPY) of employment was adopted by the Census of India for the first time in 1971. Even now there is substantial difference in perception of full employment between the GOI and the NSSO. The GOI assumes a person to be fully employed if he has 8 hours of work for a day for a lower limit of 180 days in a year. The NSSO figure is 270 days for a SPY. The SPY estimation is also not completely valid. It does not take into account the quality of employment. It was only in 1997 that a concern for quality of employment was expressed with the launching of the Revamped Public Distribution System (RPDS). It may be noted in passing that a review of the RPDS in 2000 AD has not been promising (PEO, Planning Commission, April 2001). A detailed analytical review of performance of the Indian State (1950-2000 AD) in the area of employment reveals four stages through which employment has passed wherein it is only after 1988 and specifically after 1997 that quality of employment is considered as important in State interventions. [cf A S Seetharamu: "Literacy, Employment and Social security: A Review" Working Paper No. 79, ISEC, 2001].

Food security is another important area of concern in an analysis of human rights. Poverty, food insecurity and unemployment/underemployment form an unholy triple alliance. India is facing the problem of food insecurity since independence. A Food Grains Policy Committee was appointed in 1966 which came up with an "Integrated Food Policy" wherein the need for a National Plan for supply, distribution and management of food was recognised. It recommended a four-fold strategy including a system of Public Distribution (PDS). PDS has undergone various changes. As per an analysis of food security in India, it is estimated that only 80 per cent of the poor were covered by PDS even by 1993 [A S Seetharamu, 2001]. Access to food security was out of reach of more than 60 million persons [out of 320 million persons among 870 million population by 1993]. Figures for 2002 need an estimation. It is also to been noted that starvation deaths have not been halted (the famous Kalahandi district reports from Orissa State). It may also be significant to note that among 17 major States of India, highest incidence of population below poverty line in from Orissa State. The BPL figure for 1999-2000 for Orissa State is placed at 47.15 per cent of the total population. [ES/GOI, 2002, entry on Poverty, www.nic.in]. As of today, there is surplus food production in the country. The problem is one of access, of capacity to buy food. Such a scenario had been warned by distinguished social scientists. [Raj Krishna, 1988; A.K. Sen, 1993. Note: The UNDP Human Development Report, 1998 on 'Consumption' is also eloquent on the subject]. SAP or no

SAP, the poor remain as impoverished, deprived, suffering and despondent. It needs to be noted that quality of food grains and its timely supply under PDS is not discussed in the foregoing analysis.

Another set of needs to which human beings are entitled to as their birth-right are health, education, safe drinking water, shelter and sanitation. Record of the Indian State in regard to all these needs is dismal. There is no need to review the position in regard to infant/child/ maternal mortality, illiteracy, houseless population and other variables. For considerations of space, a few other social security concerns such as old age, widowhood, physical handicaps and destitution are not reviewed in this paper.

The sum and substance of the foregoing analysis is that the performance of the Indian State in regard to realisation of human rights, specifically social and economic rights is dismal. The SAP is not by itself instrumental for the existing state of affairs. Even without SAP, the position of the common man has been pitiable. In fact, after the SAP regime, there have been increased availability of funds for the social sectors [World bank (others) funded DPEP, water supply, sanitation, housing etc; projects.] The significant questions would be: Does SAP halt the decay and help redress the dismal position in regard to realisation of human rights or does it contribute further to the state of human deprivations and to a larger spread of the despair.

Civic and Political Rights

Democracy in India has been hailed all over. It is referred to as the largest democracy in the World. It is praised for conducting periodical elections and maintaining elected governments except for a brief period of emergency rule during the 70's. Decentralised developmental planning and governance in India to the village level has also been a matter of pride and pleasure for the observer of democracy across the world. All these praises, appreciations, glorifications are good and welcome. There is no alternative to democracy whose foundations are rooted in individual rights. However, democracy in practice in India has become a euphemism and an affront on civic and political rights, though one may have reservations on the scale and magnitude of incidence. Electoral malpractices and corruption, free flight of money and muscle power, atrocities on the Dalits, marginalisation of tribal population, debilitation of persons displaced under irrigation, forestry and other development projects, custodial deaths, preventive detentions and cruelty on the detenus, are all illustrations of violations of civic and political human rights. The prevention of Atrocities of Scheduled Castes Act 1988, Electoral Code, the Criminal Procedure code, the institution of Lok Ayukta (which is a toothless roaring lion) and the like have become farcical in their operation. There is of course, a free press and mass media which is a saving grace. But the efficiency and outreach of the print and electronic media has its own limits. The sum and substance of the analysis of civic and political rights is that the record of India on human rights and human freedom is quite low in general. The total score obtained by India on Human Freedom Index Scale is 13 out of 40. [Refer UNDP HDR, 1998]. SAP has nothing to do with civic and political rights in India. This assertion is confined to realisation of individual rights.

Global Pressures

There is a global dynamics operating through the World Trade Organisation, World Intellectual Property Organisation and similar international institutions which may affect the choices of the Indian people in agriculture, industry and the services. Setting aside ethical considerations in analysis, one may cite illustrations of such international pressures: Down scaling of State subsidies, steady lowering of savings rates on term deposits in banks, dereservation of products from small scale industries sector/withdrawal of protections, privatisation of transport and telecom services, scope for multinational agencies in infrastructure development, special concessions to NRIs and for Foreign Direct Investment, tax holiday for IT companies even while they are making huge profits and paying skyrocketing salaries and perks for its top-rung personnel are noteworthy illustrations.

The global agencies and nations are powerful enough to exercise controls over the Indian economic reforms processes because of certain advantages that they enjoy and weaknesses of the Indian intellectuals. They call the shots as they are supporting nearly one-quarter of annual State expenditures in India. This support is mainly in the form of low-interest, long-term loans whose repayments are spread across future generations of Indians who are today's children. The loans survive long after those who have signed on the dotted line vanish from the planning/governing process and perish from the mother earth. A portion of this loan is used for transfer of technology, purchase of technical know-how which mainly comes in the form of foreign scholars empanelled on projects in India and for organising international seminars/ symposium/high level meetings. It is also spent for consultancy to "Indian intellectuals!" On projects in India, visits of Indian scholars abroad, visits of top bracket bureaucrats and politicians along with their delegations for project planning, feasibility meetings, signing contracts and the like. It may be noted in passing that the exorbitantly high salaries and other benefits of the Fifth Pay Commission of the Government of India, corresponding Pay Commissions of the State Governments and the UGC could be possible because of the loans. Senior civil servants of the government (IAS/IFS), central government employees, Defence personnel, Judges and the judicial officers, Railways, the university teachers, offices and employees of the State governments are enjoying a field day through the 1997 pay revisions financed through development loans from international agencies. From a position of bankruptcy in 1988 when the GOI had to pledge Gold Reserves to the Bank of England as Foreign Exchange Reserves and security for imports, Indian elite moved to a position of bankruptcy in 1988 when the GOI had to pledge Gold Reserves to the Bank of England as Foreign Exchange Reserves and security for imports, Indian elite moved to a position of plenty and prosperity by 1997, along with a new index of inflation to counterveil the spiralling price effects on the economy. Ten per cent of India's working population in the organised sector benefited at the expense of another 50 per cent working population in the unorganised sector and 40 per cent dependent population. Should you blame the SAP for this or the management of the SAP by the Indian elite? Not only has India become a debtor nation, but also there has been a easy availability of credit in all nationalised banks and other financial institutions. Attitude towards credit has been completely transformed in this country. Alternatively, developing countries like India have become a market yard for finance to the advanced countries and the agencies like the World Bank which they control. It may be worth mentioning that the United States controls 37 per cent of World's trade while the figure for India is 0.7 per cent. The US contributes 25 per cent of the regular budget of the United Nations while India contributes 0.305 per cent (2000 AD figures). The advanced countries are so prosperous (because of historical reasons, reasons which defy human ethics) that they find it difficult to manage their investment portfolios and channelise their surpluses. But for countries like India, they should have thrown their surplus wealth in the Pacific Ocean and the Mediterranean sea. It is a fact that incentives are given in the US for lowering production targets by the farmers. It is to be noted that anti-dumping laws have been formulated and adopted across the world to contain market invasion by developed countries and check economic imperialism.

Priorities in the World

Developing Countries		Advanced Countries	
Priorities	Amount Needed US$	Priorities	Amount Spent US$
Basic education for all	6 billion[a]	Cosmetics in the USA	8 billion
Water and sanitation for all	9 billion[a]	Ice cream in Europe	11 billion
Reproductive health for all women	12 billion[a]	Perfumes in Europe and the USA	12 billion
Basic health and nutrition	13 billion[a]	Pet foods in Europe and the USA	17 billion
		Business entertainment in Japan	35 billion
		Cigarettes in Europe	50 billion
		Alcoholic drinks in Europe	105 billion
		Narcotic drugs in the world	400 billion
		Military spending in the world	780 billion

a: Estimated additional annual cot to achieve universal access to basic social services in all developing countries

Source: Euromonitor 1997; UN 1997g; UNDP, UNFPA and UNICEF 1994; Worldwide Research, Advisory and Business Intelligence Services, 1997.

Source: UNDP, HDR, 1998, p. 37.

Global Divide

There is also a view that international terrorism (of which Taliban was only one example) is also a result of a global divide in human rights and human freedoms. The global divide is in four areas—Incomes, Consumption, Technology and Information.

All these 4 components go to constitute the Human Development Divide. In fact the UNDP uses two types of Human Poverty Index-HPI 1 for list and Afghanistan's rank is 89. There are 17 countries in the HP1 2 list and the rank of US is 17. [UNDP, HDR, 1998]. A table from the UNDP 1998 report is highly revealing.

How can there be even a glim prospect for realisation of human rights in the foreseeable future when there is so much of global inequality, poverty and under development?

Concluding Observations

The appalling state of human rights in India and the developing world around has little to lose or gain from the SAP. Roots of human deprivation and human distress are to be located within the basic human nature. This is essentially the perennial and unresolved philosophical problem of "the Good vs. the Evil". Justice, Equality, Freedom, Love, Compassion, Brotherhood, Tolerance are the Good while Selfishness, Greed, Prejudice, Conceit, Hatred are the Evil. Exploitation, immiserisation, deprivation, oppression, atrocities, suppression of freedoms, base materialism, imperialism, neoimperialism, manipulation, aggression, invasion, war-mongering and all the other similar behaviours are different forms of evil.

It is difficult to explain Evil in the world. Even St. Augustine who shot to fame in the world of philosophy with his Five Proofs for the existence of God failed to tackle the problem of Evil. The basic question posed to him and all the others of his tribe is: "If God is there in the world, why is there evil?", "Why does God tolerate injustice, inequality, suppression of human freedom by humans?" "Why is there so much of pain and suffering in the world?" 'Evil' has remained a mystery in philosophy

Sri Aurobindo explained evil as a transitory phenomenon. He conceived of an evolving universe wherein human society is moving towards a Superhuman society and man/woman will become a Superman/Superwomen. [Sri Aurobindo: 'Future Evolution of Man'; 'The Huan Cycle'.] Aurobindo's thesis survives historical testimony. Human society is moving towards a moral universe. Example 1: It may be noted that as recent as 130 years ago human beings were sold for a price in slave markets. Abraham Lincoln got the 'Abolition of Slavery bill' passed in US Senate in 1873, forbearing all the resistance and eventually sacrificing himself. As per the Act, compensation in cash was paid by the Government to the Slavelords who released them (just like compensation for Landlords who surrendered surplus land to the Government in India as per the Land Reforms Act). Today, slavery is unthinkable. Of course, undisclosed bonded labour is still there. Example 2: Till 1940s, famines were a recurrent phenomenon. The Royal Commission on Agriculture in India was set up in 1876 following a severe famine. The 1942 Bengal famine is the worst ever so far in recent times. There has been no famine since then in India, though there are still starvation deaths and half-starvation sufferings. Example 3: Discrimination against lowly placed caste groups, untouchability, widowhood as a curse, male chauvinism and similar evils of society were accepted as such in India till recently. At least they are now prohibited by law in organised civil society in India even though the ground realities leave much to be desired. In fact several governments of the world including India have adopted protective discrimination/affirmation policies.

One has to note that there is injustice and inequality in nature. Human beigns have no choice on their place of birth and the socio-economic background of their birth. Some are born in difficult-to-live, hilly/mountainous terrains or earth quake prone areas or cyclone/floods exposed regions; born in poor and lowly social and economic backgrounds; others are born in prosperous regions and in palace-like homes; some are granted with all the rights, privileges and freedoms at the time of their birth; others have to struggle with or without success and sacrifice quite a bit for their rights and freedoms. While there is injustice in nature, there should not be injsutice/inequality in organised human societies and in civilised life. One has to agree with Lord Robbins that "Inequality is a part of human society. It is revolting to accept it" (Lionel Robbins, 1973). (A recent review of struggles of civilised global society for human freedoms is reported in UNDP/HDR 2000 chapter 2. This annual volume is devoted to Human Rights and Development). A civilised society consists of enlightened persons. Enlightenment comprises of a faith in justice, equality and freedom as the basic Truths of life. They are the human rights. However human rights cannot be realised in a vacuum. They have to be realised in a civil society wherein there are agents who hold/control power, privileges and patronages. The agents at local/regional/national/global levels have to accept the granting of human rights as their "Perfect Duties" (usage after Immanuel Kant; 'Foundations to the Metaphysics of Morals'). Hence, it is essential to globalise the values associated with human rights (not just globalise trade and investments), globalise the ideas of democracy and individual rights before efforts are made to correct strategic interventions for human rights.

The concerned/committed intellectuals (committed for human rights), the mass media and civil society institutions have an important role to play in popularisation of the significance of human rights and human freedoms in promoting a same society. There is no use in just blaming SAP.

A Final Word

The ideas/views expressed in this article are neither a sop for the suffering humanity and those concerned with such sufferings. The need for appropriate and timely corrective on anti-people strategies for development cannot be ruled out. The thesis of this article is to promote a balanced view of SAP, to look at it across time and space, not to get disheartened and depressed by transitory events but to face reality (of SAP) boldly, resolutely, firmly, but to act with certain, circumspection and balance. The obligation to suffer grants the right to participate in decision-making and question the unwelcome effects of decisions/actions of those who are in power. Let us develop and promote a questioning culture. Such questioning has to spring from the grassroots. Intellectualism can only serve as mid-wifery for a questioning society.

4

Structural Adjustment Programme (SAP) and Human Rights

Prof. D. Narasimha Reddy

Introduction

In this paper it is proposed to examine the interrelationship between structural adjustment Progamme and human rights situation in the third world countries. Human Rights are interpreted in a larger sense as right to live with human dignity.

The emphasis in this session is on the basic Components of certain economic systems which ensured the right to level with our dependence but with self respect.

The first part of the paper is devoted to explaining the meaning of the Structural Adjustment Programme (SAP). The second part deals with the implications of Structural Adjustment Programme in terms of the livelihood activities, and social consumption of particularly the poor section. The third part deals with the experience of structural adjustment in some of the less developed countries where it has been operated from 1990's. The fourth part discusses the nature of intervention contemplated and their inadequacy.

Structural Adjustment Programme (SAP)

There is a certain amount of conscious vagueness in the concept of structural adjustment. It is often used in the context of "Global Transformation". Global transformation is defined as "Integration of the national economies different countries into a global system of Production, consumption and trade", and for the developing countries it would especially signify trade and investment liberalisation in the immediate period and domination as a art of long term adjustments. One can easily understand that structural adjustment here is meant as an adjustment of the economies of the less developed countries to suit the changes taking place in the highly developed capitalist countries. Structural adjustment, therefore, may be seen as having three important dimensions:

(i) In the case of external sector, adjustment from the existing system of protected trade towards free trade and investment,

(ii) In internal economy, adjustment in the form of shift from an economic organisation dominated by the public sector towards the primacy of private sector, and

(iii) In production structure, adjustment from emphasis on capital goods production to that of consumption goods production.

The rational for structural adjustment programme is provided by referring to the inefficiencies of public sector, the inappropriateness of protected trade and the unsuitability of factor endowments in less developed countries for the production of capital goods. Structural adjustment, is equated with privatisation and free trade which together are supposed to bring about improved efficiency, competitiveness, and faster growth. What is of interest here is the fact that India before independence did possess all the three structural elements of being dominated by private sector, free trade and an industrial sector confined largely to consumer goods. But there were hardly any elements of competitiveness, efficiency and faster growth. It only helps us to see why there is criticism of SAP as shift to a kind of new colonialism!

The typical components of an orthodox structural adjustment programme are macroeconomic policies of fiscal austerity, monetary contraction and devaluation at one level, and sectoral and microeconomic policies at a second level. The second set of policies is characterised by the deregulation of labour markets, financial markets. And agricultural process and removal of trade barriers. A related goal is to minimise the most efficient producer. It is widely documented that adjustment policies such as currency devaluation, price deregulation, privatisation, export strategies and the removal of subsidies of food and health services leave large sections of the poor in adjusting countries poorer in that short-run.

Now let us examine the impact of the structural adjustment programme on Human Rights. One of the widely expected consequences of structural adjustment programme is the rise in prices of food grains and other food products. Food prices are expected to increase for the following reasons:

(i) Reduction in the subsidy of agricultural inputs like fertilizers will push prices of food grains.

(ii) The rise in the prices of procurement of food grains may affect the food prices even under the public distribution system.

(iii) The devaluation of currency that goes with the restricting of real value of domestic currency as a part of adjustment programme will make the impact expensive and raise the prices of domestic commodities.

(iv) The external trade liberalisation in the case of agricultural commodities may lead to export of some of the food grains and result in increased prices of food grains, and

(v) The rising fuel and freight costs will lead to welfare losses for the poor.

All these upward changes in the prices of essential commodities would directly affect the poorer sections and deprive them of adequate consumption of essential commodities.

Unemployment

In addition to the rising prices, SAP will lead to retrenchment of workers particularly in the organised sector in the name of "exit policy". The compensation, provided to the retrenched may not alleviate the problem much under the adjustment programme, there is no indication of rise in employment in the immediate future. If at all there is any increase in employment, it may be confined to some informal activities. Here is also a feeling that some of the employment in the organised sector will be actually transformed into unorganised sector. The loss of jobs, the loss of security available for those in jobs and the non-availability of new employment opportunities together are likely to cause serious distress to workers' interest. Low and falling household incomes are a chronic problem for poor people in poor societies. These chronic conditions are often accentuated following recession and adjustment as unemployment and wages fall and food prices rise. For instance in India, the adjustment impact of employment took two forms viz, work-force reduction, either involuntary through retrenchment or through rarely retirement incentive and worker safety-net mechanism leading to some form of unemployment benefit scheme. Lack of Proper conceptualisation and implantation have caused a lot of hardship to many workers who lost their jobs in sick industries as well as other industries.

Social Deprivation

The adjustment programme in the name of fiscal constraint is likely to affect public expenditure in all sectors including the social sector. The process of privatisation is likely to extend beyond production sectors, into the social sector. There would be increase in the privatisation of education, health, rural infrastructure like drinking water facilities and urban infrastructure like better sanitation. The philosophy of charging for the social services, may deprive access to better health and educational facilities to the poorer sectors.

The experience of SAP in many countries of Africa and Latin America where is was introduced in 1980s shows that there has been extensive deprivation. The UN organisations like UNICEF had accumulated evidence from various countries that women and children suffered the most, especially those with poorest social status, in 1980s where the structural adjustment programme was implemented. The Human Development Reports have been referring to SAP as the one which emphasises market driven growth which leads to "job less, worthless, voiceless, rootless and future less growth". The SAP does not favour equity in redistribution, both between, and within the countries. It shows that the globalised market economy has over the last 15 years deepened the economic polarisation between developed and developing countries. Only 15 countries registered improved growth and income during the period, while nearly 100 have shown negative rates of economic growth and per income during the period, while nearly 100 have shown negative rates of economic growth and per capita income. In 70 of these countries average income was lower than it has been in 1980, and in 43 countries lower than in 1970, the difference in income between the developing and industrialised world trippled between 1970-1993. Even a World Bank study in 1996 on social dimensions of adjustment which analyzed 53 adjusting countries concludes that only 60% of these countries could reduce poverty and inequalities.

While it is generally clear that the poor suffer extensively because of Adjustment Programme, women appear to be the worst suffers. There has been disproportionate cost of adjustments borne by women which violates their rights of development guaranteed in national and international conventions. Adjustment programmes have caused erosion and suspension of the rights of large sections of the poor, of whom the great majority are women. A Commonwealth Expert (1989) summarized the impact of adjustments as follows: "Women are at the centre of the crisis and bear the brunt of the adjustment efforts. It is women who are severely affected by the deteriorating incomes and prices, and who have desperately sought means to survive. It is women who had to find extra work to supplement family income; it is women who have rearranged family budgets...and it is women who have been most immediately affected by cuts in health and educational facilities and by the rising stability and death among the children. Women are at the front line of the crisis in the developing world and it is they who have most severely been affected and have had the greatest responsibility for adjustment of their lives to ensure survival."

Evidence from several countries shows that austerity is a female responsibility. Men maintain their social and personal expenditures, while women are expected to make ends meet with fewer resources, by working longers hours within and outside the home.

Economic stagnation and decline exacerbate gender inequality in household situation as well. In societies where anti-female dissemination is endemic, as in South Asia, women usually eat the last and least, and girl children are also poorly fed. In times of poverty and in substance crisis, their already poor nutritional status is worsened because women have to reduce their share of food to maintain that of their husbands, and girls get even less food than they normally would. Poverty compounded by reduction in food subsidies under an adjustment programme thus disproportionately affects female consumption within the household.

Even the short period of experience in the case of India suggests that the rising prices, the increasing pressure on subsidies to public distribution system, the limited allocation to education, and health facilities have actually tended to worsen the situation of poverty in India.

Adjustment with Human Face

The consequences of SAP in affecting the well being of the poor in the poorest countries is not surprising even at the very beginning of this programme conceived by the World Bank and IMF. The UNICEF argued that the programme would adversely affect the poorer sections and pleaded, for an adjustment within human face. As a result, certain "safety nets" had to be evolved along with the structural adjustment programme. At least three such "safety nets" could be identified. First, prices, especially of food articles, were expected to rise necessitating the supply of food at subsidized prices through the public distribution system to the poorer sections. Second, the adjustment programme was not expected to bring about any rise in opportunities of productive employment to the poor. On the contrary, it was expected to lead to actual retrenchment through "Exit Policy". To soften the impact of adverse effect, the "safety nets" are to be provided in the form of Mass Public Employment Programmes. Third, the fiscal crunch which affected public expenditure on social sector had to be readjusted in favour of services which benefit the poor. In education the "safety nets" concerned were that the limited resources would be devoted more to "elementary and lower, secondary level". In health, the resources would be used more for preventive health care.

The implementation of the safety nets have been fraught with severe constraints of resources, inability to poverty target the beneficiary groups, lack of properly conceived public works programmes and half-hearted efforts to provide health and education facilities to the poorer section. The consequences of all these effects had been one of growing deprivation of the poorest of the poor whose very right to life with dignity stands seriously jeopardized. A focus on the human rights implications of market driven growth is necessary also to challenge the current trend in industrialised countries to undermine the role of the UN in human development while ceding greater power and authority to the World bank and IMF.

Conclusion

SAP by emphasising market induced growth leaves several vulnerable sections like women, weaker sections and the poor in general, excluded from the benefits of growth. In fact, often these marginalised nations and groups appear to suffer worse deprivation of their basic rights like secure employment and stable income. The withdrawal of the state from the responsibility of promoting inclusive growth results in severe hardship to the poor wherever they are.

5

Structural Imbalances–Courts Role in Strengthening Human Right Jurisprudence

Prof. E. Vijaya Kumar

The society is an unequal structure. Some have power over others and some have more access to resources than others. The power is not merely physical, but also social, cultural ideological; and the resources are not merely material but also cultural. This inequality is indeed the source of most demands of rights...This is equality also inhibited the achievements of rights and thus results in conflict between various groups in the society. Human rights struggle and movements aims to realise the Human right objectives. In reality, Human right movement requires further struggle, both inside and outside the courts, for the actual realisation of those rights which society has officially accepted as part of its law, as part of the legitimate status quo, but which are powerfully resisted by the holders of power and privilege within society.

'Human Rights' and 'human rights law' have become familiar expressions in recent years. The expression human rights refers to a wide range of rights, some of them directly guaranteed in the law and the Constitutions, some of them inferred through the elaboration of legal and constitutional provisions by the higher Courts, and some that exist is yet only at level of political belief and expression and are yet to achieve the status of law. These rights include the Constitutional fundamental rights pertaining to life and liberty (civic, political and religions), the rights against untouchability and forced labour, protection to minorities and socially disadvantaged sections (dalits, women and advisasis), etc, the rights in criminal law that ensure protection against forcible extraction of confessions and a fair and reasonable procedure for the investigation and trial of criminal offences, the rights of workers elaborated in labour and industrial legislation; the rights of women to maintenance and protection from marital harassment and physical abuse at the hands of men; the rights of dalits and adviasis against mental; and physical abuse by dominant, pollution-free environment; the right of children against abuse of their tender age in hazardous employment; and so on. None of these rights is as completely guaranteed in the law as one would wish and all of them are abused frequently in practice, and yet they are not without substance.

Human rights are constantly asserted in the Courts and in society; and they are frequently sought to be extended, against both in the political sphere and the Courts of Law.

Today, the notion of human rights has expanded to an extent where it connotes a range of egalitarian social, political and economic aspirations. The aspirations that one finds expressed in social and political debate and agitation to well beyond what is conceded by the law, at any given point of time. And yet the struggle for the aspirations goes on. Often it is expressed in the form of a demand for the amendment of the law to incorporate the aspiration as a right. Such a recognition of rights by the law inaugurates a double legitimacy, the claim to those rights acquries juridical legitimacy, and the law to that extent acquries an enhanced moral legitimacy. The rights are then easier to enjoy, and the law is then worthy of greater respect.

The judicial interpretation that has, in the Indian context, progressively expanded the human rights content of the law. Unlike other branches of Indian law, where statutory provisions outstrip judge made law'. In the matter of human rights, whatever law we have owes more to the Courts than to the legislatures; or atleast as much. It cannot be said that thereby the India Courts have created a paradise of rights, far from it.

The source of the progress in the law is closely linked to actual progress in social relations and the social situation.

In a society ridden with several factors contributing to social imbalance of the law remained, a notoriously conservative. It acts to preserve and reproduce the relations (social, economic and political) of the status quo. Yet, that is not a fatal defect. For when new aspirations arise in society, the law first works against them, but if they succeed in fighting and making themselves part of the social structuie, if they put enough pressure upon society to accept them as legitimate aspirations, the law then proceeds to define the aspirations in legal terms and incorporate them within the law. It then proceeds to preserve and reproduce these new aspirations too in theory, then, the progressive change too becomes part of the (new) status quo, and the law by its very conservative nature must protect the new status quo too. The change thus becomes juristically legitimate. By this means it not only helps in the day to day realisation of the newly achieved aspirations, but also helps, by strengthening the democratic culture of society to the extent of the newly institutionalized right, to achieve further change in a progressive direction.

An attempt is made in this paper to explain the role played by the courts in standardising the norms to equalized the unequal or mitigate hardship caused to them in a given circumstances.

1. State is duty Bound to Protect inmates of jail

Duty of police to guard jail—Failure or negligence—Under trial prisoners in jail apprehending danger to their life and requesting authorities to take extra safety measurement. No action taken thereon—Police constables on duty found not vigilant-Miscreants entering sub-jail with help of ladder at night time and hurling bombs at inmates, under trial prisoners—police to guard jail properly and to ensure safety of prisoners as required under R48 [Para 13].

[See: Chella Ramakrishna Reddy and others vs. State of Andhra Pradesh by District Collector, Kurnool, A.I.R. 1989 A.P. 235.

2. Speedy trial and release of under trial prisoners who were in jail for longer period directed

FIR should not be quashed in every case where a person is detained in custody during pre-trial stage beyond 90 days and change sheet is not filed—Enforcement of personal liberty under Art. 21 can been ensured only by speedy trial—Courts shall therefore make an endeavour to ensure speedy trial of under-trial prisoners—Detention of under-trial prisoners in jail for longer periods than the maximum term they would have been sentenced if convicted, amounts to violation of Art. 21-Such under-trial prisoners have to be released forthwith—A list of accused who should be released appended to judgement Charge-sheets against the accused shown in the appendix quashed—Directions given to concerned judges to expenditure disposal of cases against other accused charged for grievous offence—Directions also given to follow guidelines mentioned by Supreme Court in A.I.R. 1979 S.C. 1360 is releasing the under-trial prisoners in cases other than those mentioned in Appendix.

[See : Nallapareddy Prasanna Kumar Reddy Vs State of Andhra Pradesh rep. by Principal Secretary, Home Department, Hyderabad and others. 1994 (1) A.L.T. 684

(D.B)=1994 Cr.L.J.2016 (A) (A.P)]

3. Principles of Natural Justice Applicable to Prison Offences:

Conviction for jail offence viz. For surrendering late by accused released on parole—Order of punishment passed by Superintendent of Jail—Confirmation of punishment without hearing accused is violative of principles of natural justice.

[See : Haiderkhan Lalhan Pathan Vs State of Gujarat and others. 199 Cr.L.J. 1266(Gujarat)]

4. Prisoners Entitled to Wages not Lesser Than Minimum Wages.

Wage earnings—Prisoners—Entitled to get reasonable wages not below "minimum wages" prescribed by Minimum Wages Act—Wage earning scheme prescribing remuneration less than minimum wages-Amounts to "Forced Labour" and as such violative of Art. 23.

Prisoners—Entitled to get reasonable wages, not below "minimum wages" prescribed under Minimum Wages Act.

Fundamental Rights of Prisoners—Extinction, is not total Prisoners, entitled to get wages not below minimum wages.

[See : Gurdev Singh and others etc. Vs State of Himachal Pradesh and others. 1992 Cr.L.J 2542 (A) (H.P)]

5. State to Compensate Wife for Suicide of Husband Jailed for :

Compensation—Payment of, as palliative measure-Husband not paying maintenance amount to wife-Husband arrested—Committing suicide in jail—State, as palliative measure, directed to pay compensative to wife.

Maintenance—Non-payment of—Arrest of husband, who committed suicide in jail—Liability to pay compensation to wife.

[See : Mrs. Selvam and another Vs State of Tamil Nadu and others 1994 Cr.L.J.N.O.C.35 (Madras).]

6. Concept of Cruelty.

Maintenance—'cruelty'—Husband underwent sterilisation operation before marriage—Concealed this fact from wife—Thereby, forcing wife to be barren—Act of husband amounts to cruelty in all aspects—Wife entitled to stay apart and claim maintenance.

7. Police Officer Denied Bail in Dowry Death.

Bail-Accused a Police officer-Allegation of committing death of his wife for dowry—Evidence of eye witnesses that accused severely beat deceased and bungled her head against wall—Medial evidence that death was due to head injury—Evidence to show that there was demand for dowry—Accused cannot be said to be innocent—Not entitled to bail particularly so because accused is police officer and the eye witnesses are residing in same locality.

[See : Immamuddin Vs. The State of others. 1994 Cr.L.J N.O.C. 324 (Delhi).]

8. No Leniency in Rape and Murder Case:

Sentence—Rape and murder case—Offence of rape and murder alleged to be committed by accused—Has been proved by testimonies of all eye—witnesses and also corroborated by medicinal barbaric—Not a fit case for showing leniency in sentence [Para 15]

[See : Jagat Bahadur Vs State of Himachal Pradesh. 1994 Cr.L.J 3396 (B) (H.P)]

9. Outraging Modesty is not Trifle:

Quashing of-alleged act of top most official of State Police in slapping senior Lady officer on her posterior in presence of gathering of elite of society—In fact situation amounting in outraging of modesty of Lady Officer—Nothing in FIR that all alleged act was committed accidentally or by mistake or it was slip—Allegations in FIR making out offences under Ss.354 and 509, I.P.C —Offence relating to modesty of woman not being trivial—Section 95 of I.P.C. not attracted—Quashing of F.I.R and complaint by High Court—illegal especially in absence of finding that allegations made in F.I.R were absurd and inherently improbable. [Paras 17,21,23,24]

B.R. Bajaj vs. State of Punjab and others 1996 Cr.L.J.381 (A) (S.C.)]

10. Harassment of women at work place

11. Problem of Dowry

12. Noise pollution is infringement of right to life

Right to life—Public meeting—Use of loud speaker—Exposure of unwilling persons to dangerous and disastrous levels of noise—Amounts of infringement of right to life.

Right to life—Noise pollution—Exposure of unwilling person to dangerous and disastrous levels of noise—infringes right to life.

[See : P.A Jacob Vs. The Superintendent of Police Kottayam and another A.I.R 1993 Kerala]

13. Closure of Industries for Pollution Control:

Water pollution—Public interest litigation—Tanneries discharging effluent in Ganga and not setting up primary treatment plant in spite of being asked to do so for several years, not caring to put in appearance to express willingness to set up pre-treatment plant—Order directing than to stop working their tanneries issued.

[See :M.C. Mehta Vs. Union of India and others. A.I.R 1899 S.C. 1037.]

14. Compensation for Man Missing:

Where the police had taken into custody an individual for interrogation for his alleged involvement in a double murder case but thereafter his whereabouts were not known and the police failed to give any satisfactory explanation; held in the circumstances, the wife of the detenue is entitled to compensation for the harm done to her and her family as a result of the unlawful acts of the instrumentalities of the state.

[See : Lalitha Vs Director General of Police, Madras. A.P.L.J 1989 (2) 84 (D.N.C) (D.B) = 1989 A.P.L.J (Crl) 434.]

15. Duty of Doctors in Accident Cases:

Public Interest Litigation—Professional ethics of medical profession—Injured citizen brought for medical treatment—Should instantaneously be given medial aid and thereafter procedural criminal law should be allowed to operate—There is no legal impediment for doctor to attend to such cases immediately.

Accident cases—Medical treatment—Duty of doctor to attend—Procedural criminal law no bar.

Injured citizen—Medical treatment—Duty of doctor.

[See: Paramanand Katara Vs. Union of India and others. 1990 Cr.LJ 671 (S.C)=A.I.R 1089 S.C. 2039.]

In addition to these, a few principles, in the area of woman and children, are also worthy of mention like.

(a) The evidence of corroboration is unnecessary in case of rape of prosecutrix by police officer.

(b) Where police officer committed rape on young girl in her late teens the court observe no sympathy or petty on the police officer and punishment award was exemplary on Nature.

(c) No leniency in sentencing in bride burning cases

(d) Bail refused to police accused of custodial gang rape.

(e) Blood test impermissible to rebut paternity in maintaining proceedings.

In India the courts have ,thus, played a role of modulator to adjust the in requilibrium existing in social fabric. Thus interpretation techniques adopted by the courts and incorporation of international and human rights covenants to expand the amplitude of provision strengthens the Human rights jurisprudence

6

Positivisation of Human Rights and Responsibilities–A 21st Century Challenge

Prof. A. Lakshminath

An activist State is one which takes interest in all forms of the activities of their subjects sometimes leading to undue interference. Presently most of the countries are very conscious of the Crises of 'ungovernability'. To adopt to the new structure of Societies governments have chosen to delegalise and deregulate and often transfer most of the state's dominant sphere to the private. The old sovereign states shrunk largely in the process of regionalisation as well as globalisation. These in total given a picture of diminishing state. What we should learn from this unanticipated paradigm shift at the beginning of the millennium, especially developing countries, endeavouring to achieve better levels of economic and political living without repeating the whole dialectic process?.

While constitution is the process by which the governmental action is effectively restrained and is understood as the process of the function of which it is not only to organise but to restrain, Constitutionalism refers to limits on majority decisions, more specifically to limits that are in some sense self-imposed. Constitutionalism in both an end and means. It is both value—free and value—loaded. It has both normative and empirical dimensions.

1. **Diminishing States:** Because of gloablisation, besides the increase of massive transborder exchange and interaction relations in economic, cultural and information exchange processes including cross-border transmission of pollutants, more and more non-governmental factors are operating at a transnational level quite independently of sovereign states. This is followed by the progressive loss of power of those states in the process of becoming democratic.

Decisions involving States are taken outside government Institutions which ultimately leads to national deregulation and Privatisation. The interaction of the outside and inside elements accelerates the diminishing of States. The role of the World Bank in recent times was controversial for the financial turbulence it created in East Asia.

2. **Challenge to Basic Human Rights:** The fundamental rights are not just constitutionally, "Proclaimed" but also "Protected". The normative context of some liberty-rights, going beyond the "subjective" right includes institutional guarantee. The constitutional rights can be jeopardised if proclaimed rights like dignified existence, Medicare, education, livable environment etc. are not properly met or resources adequately distributed.

3. **Third Way:** The thesis of 'More market, less State' and the anti-thesis of the Constitutional call for social solidarity and Welfare seem to merge into a synthesis. The object of fundamental rights should expand to all those who share the State's responsibility either this way or that way.

The Govt. is small but clever. It gives up costly micro social intervention, but in its place promotes macro-social stability and progress. Its success relies very much on the experience of regulation, knowing exactly when and where it should obtain from intervention. Communities must be strong and willing to share States responsibility. In short, this synthesis pre-supposes, practising experience of both liberal and social democracy. If the State has never been strong further shrinkage of Govt. will only make it weaker.

4. **Internationalisation of Human Rights:** States are not diminishing but emergency human rights problems are becoming big.

The term human rights is vague and ill defined. Human Rights are those minimal rights which every individual must have by virtue of his being 'a member of human family'. The desirability of human rights as fundamental rights overlooks the fact that rights are not fundamental in one historical epoch is not so in another time and place. Kant's prophetic concept of History' and Maines "Status to contract" emphasise transformation of ideas from society to individualist concept of society and, therefore, of the State This is in opposition to the much more solid and ancient concept of society as an organic whole more important than the constituent part (Gestalt).

The European Court of Human Rights established under European convention on Human rights 1953, played an important role during 60's and 70's. The Court has become the constitution Court of Europe with the collapse of the Soviet Union. Vienna declaration (14-25 June) 1993 succeeded for the first time in the recognition and reaffirmation of the interdependence between democracy, development and human rights and human rights and the Universality, indivisibility and interdependence of human rights.

5. Re-Institutionalisation of basic rights. One thousand years of history of human rights development has centred on the stage of Sovereign States where governments and citizens pulled and pushed each other. What we need at this juncture is the reinstitutionalisation of human rights protection to adopt to the more and more differentiated and complicated post modern social frame work, which includes identification of judicially accountable objects of human rights, recognition and facilitation of access rights to social net work of all kind and strengthening of international Co-operation on this subject.

While the State in a liberal democracy is limited to the role of a faithful night—watcher, its counter part in a social democracy is expected to be an omnipotent caretaker, at best from cradle to the grave. It is within the discourse on rights, that responsibility of the individuals towards other individuals and perhaps towards the State are a new challenge. With the Universal Proclamation of Human rights in the 20th Century, the evolution of the idea of human Rights seem to have been completed. Human rights have evolved into Universally applicable norms. The self-evident status of human rights seems to have come to an end. The belief that human beigns not only have human rights but also duties and responsibilities deserve more attention from scholars.

Constitutionalism or Rule of law and democracy are the central pillars of Govt. Liberalism has become the triumphant ideology which is no longer challenged by rival ideologies.

Most of the former communist countries have adopted constitutions passed on Democracy and Rule of Law. Consequently, increasing globalisation coupled with decreasing attention to the national sovereign state has taken place. Later half of last century demonstrated Universal acceptance of constitutionalism and democracy. Constitutional law is based on theories of rights.

The declaration of human responsibilities focuses attention on alternative moral prospective which may lead to a reconsideration of the place of duties and responsibilities in constitutional law. While liberalism stresses the idea of individual liberty and entailing rights. Communitarians underline the importance of community, solidarity and responsibility. Communitarians are a group of ethical scholars, social philosophers and social scientists who came together in Washington DC in 1990 for the first time. Two important features of liberal tradition are

(1) Priority of rights and 2) government's neutrality between competing conceptions of what is good in life or which way of life is morally preferable. On September 1997, the Interaction council published a Universal Declaration of Human Responsibilities as a Counter part to the Universal declaration of Human Rights. Thus we should not only strive for Liberty and Equality but also for Fraternity and Solidarity. Human Rights indicates where Govt. Action should end and where the private sphere of the individual begins. Duties and responsibilities by themselves do not constitute state limits. Responsibilities can be regarded as being constitutional norms. Against this background the challenge to the 21st Century is to balance the human rights with human responsibilities which is delicate indeed. It is the judiciary which also con successfully meet the Challenge in positivising the Human rights and Human Responsibilities.

7

Human Rights and Judiciary

Dr. D. Venkateswarlu

This seminar seeks to focus on 'Human Rights—Challenges for the 21st Century'. It is the rights that are challenged anyway. Obviously, the issue of human rights is a very sensitive one. However, I would like to exercise my right as a citizen (under Article 19 a), and also fulfil my responsibility as a social scientist to express my opinions on issues of central concern to all of us. This is only a general presentation and, I am afraid, not a focused one any particular issue. It was indeed a great event this morning when eminent jurists addressed various issues relating to human rights.

The legislature, the judiciary and the executive are said to be the three important organs of the State. We have seen the functioning and efficacy of all these three institutions over the last fifty-one years. In popular perception, the legislature and seecutive have not lived unto expectations and aspirations of the people.

The legislature, an important instrument in a democracy, is accountable to none. The way decisions of a small section of a party's leadership gets carried as that of the party itself, and built—dozing of the same in legislative for a has brought down the House in the esteem of the people. Further, thanks to the media exposures, both in print and electronic, we know what all methods that the politicians do not hesitate to use to get elected to different' representative bodies. I believe that we all should seriously take cognizance of an ever—increasing and dangerous phenomenon, which may perhaps be called usurping of democracy' by vested interests. Democracy, at least in our context, has only come to mean capture of power by any means albeith through the balbt box. Doesn't matter what the means—preventing the poor and low from exercising their right to franchise (a serious violation of the rights of citizenship—Articles 5—11), influencing them with parochial factors of region, religion, caste and others, buying their votes with money and liquor, if not others. Means is never important, it is only the end—that of capturing power. Democracy is mauled and assaulted in so many ways that unless we wake up at least now and restore it onto track, the derailment may not be much later. I think we all agree that there is no alternative to democracy. We have to jealously safeguard before it gets lost to the posterity.

The executive has proved to be not only inadequate and incompetent, but also irresponsible. They are happy to only toe the line of the party in power forgetting their basic loyalty to the constitution of the country. It is a pity how low even some all-India service officers (supposed to a very bright lot) can come down to serve their career interests and personal ambitions. How unrealistic and self-centred the executive can be has become manifest in the recent years. I am referring to their total ignorance, indifference and apathy to disinvestment in and privatisation of PSUs. They failed to realise that it would soon embrace the services of the government itself. We are already witnessing it in the fields of education and health. Others may not be far. In due course, one need not be shocked if the governance itself is put in the hands of corporate giants for efficiency and profit-making'.

In these circumstances, judiciary is being looked at as the only hope to correct and reverse some of the unfortunate trends setting in our country. Neither the power of the mighly nor the indiscreet threats of the aggressors have so far influenced it. There are many instances when the government or the individuals, however highly placed they might be, had to bend on their knees in various courts of law and were forced to abide by the law and the rule-book. They have spoken and acted in defence of the poorest of the poor on more than one occasion.

But, of late, one is distressed to learn some unfortunate instances of error in judgements. One is remained of a case in which a learned High Curt judge refused to get convinced about the rape of a Dalit victim by high-caste youth in spite of corroborative evidence. One only hopes such (un)learned judges are only odd men out. One also notes with sadness the prolonged litigation, which goes against the interests of the poor, helpless and powerless.

From a sociological point of view, the judiciary cannot be viewed in subtract. The jurists hail from a particular social and economic background. Consequently, they inherit the value system and mind-set of their socio-economic group. It takes a strong rational re-orientation to recast their beliefs and value system, and to develop an objective perspective in sitting over judgements. Many, many judges have proved that they have such an objective perspective. May such tribe increase in leaps and bounds.

If I could make an uncalled for suggestion, I would plead for dropping such colonial forms of addresses like 'Your Lordship'. The Americal form of the same Mr. Justice' sounds rational and democratic.

HUMAN RIGHTS: LABOUR AND ENVIRONMENT

8

Core Labour Standards, Human Rights and Structural Adjustments: The Indian Experience and Perspectives

Prof. G. Saibaba

This paper collects arguments developed in favour of and against labour standards and human rights. It is divided into five sections. The first section examines international core labour standards and develop their major justifications as well as the real arguments against them. The second section discusses the basic human rights and its correlation with core labour standards. The third section provides the much needed information and evolution of structural adjustment programme and its challenges and also the ideological grounds of Structural Adjustment Programme in counter revolution in development thinking. Today 'Counter Revolution' has became the ideological basis for Structural Adjustment Programme in a way. Section four attempts to present and review the impact of core labour standards and human rights on the economics of the third world countries. Section five deals with the challenges poled by structural changes on these two-core labour standards and human rights. Further an attempt has also been made to probe the policy implications of structural adjustment programme and the vision of these adjustments in this century.

SECTION—I

The word 'Labour standards' is used in two ways: descriptively and normatively. Used descriptively they indicate us the actual terms of employment, quality of work and wellbeing of workers at any specific time and place. Used normatively both labour standards and human rights specify and stipulate normative rules. Basically they represent the common understanding or understanding between labour and employer, between different sections of society. Generally Labour standards and Human Rights as conventions or recommendations adopted by the international labour conference following an elaborate procedure for standard setting and their translations into conventions and recommendations. Human Rights are presented in Universal declaration of human rights for the year 1948 and the two covenants one on civil and social rights, second on social and economic rights of 1966 and subsequent U.N. Conventions.

The controversy between the neo-classical economists and neo-institutionalists provide the arguments for an against core labour standards. The neo-classical economists regarded labour standards as 'Rigidity which hinders the employer from adjusting his output and employment to changes in demand and technology. Therefore they conclude that Labour Standards are redundant at best and harmful at worst. Thus the neo-classical paradigm treats trade unions, collective bargaining and Labour Standards which may rise the terms and conditions of employment above what would be under competition. Therefore this paradigm is anti-theatrical to International Labour Organisation philosophy and ignore the value of Labour Standards as an instrument of social change. The neo-institutionalists defended Labour Standards and institutions on the basis of their contributions to productive efficiency and social justice.

The neo-classical economists from developing countries expressed their fear that internationally imposed Labour Standards will be a veil for protectionism, and will close off export appropriate for developing countries. The neo-institutional perspective advocates finaling the appropriate levels and kind of regulation to facilitate operation of economically dynamic and socially acceptable national and international labour markets.

Three Types of Core Labour Standards

Core Labour Standards have been classified in many ways. Sengen Berger stated three types of bour Standards.

1. Standard of protection which include International Labour Organisation conventions and recommendations relating to seven important aspects of protection such as working time, standards ensuring occupational health and safety, loss if job, minimum wage regulations, equality of opportunity, protection of particular groups of workers and protection from forced and bonded labour.

2. Standards of participation (Standards of participation provide the rights and means required for the joint setting and implementation of Labour Standards by employer, worker and government in the process of restructuring.

3. Standards of promotion. Standard of promotion are defined as these which further increases the productivity of labour. They promote creation of employment, combat unemployment and underemployment and finance functioning of the labour marks. A long list of standards of promotion has been developed by International Labour

Organisation. Sengen Berger emphasized a package role of Labour Standards, each standard being complementary to the other[1]

International Labour Organisation and Labour Standard

International Labour Organisation (ILO) was created at the end of first world war in 1919. In response to the harshness of working conditions during the industrial revolution in most countries participating in trade dominated by the colonial based global trading systems. The demand for regulations of labour and employment conditions was particularly based on humanitarian foundations. The International Labour Organisation is the forum for dialogue between governments, employers and unions to achieve the fundamental objective of raising labour and social standards as integral element of national economic development. Various GATT negotiations and agreements culminating in WTO in 1995 has created a challenge to the International Labour Organisation under vastly different conditions. The sudden collapse of the Soviet Union also has important bearings on the emerging consensus pertaining to labour standards. In recent years two significant debates have occurred around International Labour Organisation conventions: one related to the issue of the relationship between the conventions and trade, and the other to the concept of "Core Labour Standards". It is now generally accepted that the core Labour Standards are related to:

(a) freedom of association and the right to collectively bargain,

(b) elimination of forced labour,

(c) equality and absence of all forms of discrimination, and

(d) abolition of child labour.

The International Labour Organisation operates through development of conventions approved by members at the

International Labour Conference. It is for the government to ratify individual conventions. After ratification this should become part of their national law and governments must report to the International Labour Organisation on the application of a signed convention (failure to implement, failure to enforce) and these are viewed by a technical panel (committee of experts). Breaches of convention or publicised and can bring publicity and moral pressure to bear on countries which fail to meet the International Labour Organisation's requirements after ratification of a convention. In fact the International Labour Organisation conventions are voluntary and there are no penal sanctions for not fulfilling the requirements of the conventions this means that they are soft laws but the reporting and monitoring requirements make them much more serious or harder international instruments than those developed by other United Nations agencies (ex. UNICEF). Now there has been a long term tendency for countries to be move cautious in signing new conventions and declarations. This tendency is particularly noticeable with the International Labour Organisation where no convention established since 1976 has attracted only fifty rectifications from the 173 member countries and none adopted in the last ten years has attracted 25[2].

The slow down in ratification in recent years was partly the result of growing opposition to International Labour Organisation standards setting from employer in both developed and developing nations and specially governments in developing countries. The collapse of communism and the end of cold war made many employers doubt the value of the International Labour Organisation, and government form developing countries felt International Labour Organisation standards has reduced their competitive edge. However International Labour Organisation has obtained a new leased of life due to strong support from the United States administration in recent years, as a by-product of the world trade organisation. Now a trade linked labour class enforceable for penalties and sanctions as part of the WTO, led many employees and governments to reappraise the role of International Labour Organisation in the debate on Labour Standards, worker's rights and human rights. In particular, Labour practices, which might have give countries an unfair advantage fin trade, have been the subject of close attention of the International Labour Organisation.

In this context child labour along with freedom of association, freedom from forced labour, according to Chaudhari, "has been at the Centre of the International Labour Organisation's push for commitment to a set of core Labour Standards. This has given child labour activists new hope for effective multilateral action to eliminate child labour".[3] The fulfilment of basic rights requires performance by some individuals/institutions of atleast three kinds of duties:

(i) duties to avoid depriving,

(ii) duties to product children from deprivation and

(iii) duties to protect and aid the deprived.

A duties driven system with legally enforceable rights is the only way out. Enlightened civil societies can create public opinion that will force the pace of legal and social change in their respective domains.

SECTION—II

Basic Human Rights

The UNO and its specialised agenings, (Specially ILO, FAO) starting with the declaration of universal human rights in 1948 have pursued the issue of human rights and the associated core Labour Standards. In recent years, particularly since the inception of WTO, ideas pertaining to the issue of human rights have acquired a life and the potency of their own and the United Nation's search for an unambiguous role, a paradigm shift is unfolding. Indian policy makers in recent years have been dissenting to the emerging international agenda on the subject somewhat apologetically. The Indian contribution on the subject are original and rooted in our idealistic tradition. Here we propose to explore the subject from an Indian perspective. They are 30 types of human rights listed in various documents. Out focus is to integrate human rights with core Labour Standards in an emerging structural adjustment programme.

Indian Perspective Nobel laureate Amartya Kumar Sen spear headed a global paradigm shift in thinking on the causes of absolute poverty and famine, in addition to providing conceptual clarity on the issues of measurement. Sen has presented the link between the capabilities and entitlement as well as the community effects, particularly in the content of gender bias and school education with similar clarity and force. He has enlightened the role of democracy and freedom of press in ensuring desired outcome on human rights issues. The trinity articulated by Sen, namely freedoms, capabilities and entitlements are at the heart of human rights and core Labour Standards.[4] Sen named the East Asian strategy of development as the Eastern Strategy.[5] Which, he maintains, is based on ancient wisdom and a high degree of pragmatism.

The preamble of the constitution of India and the section on directive principle of the state policy formulated during 1946-49 and adopted in January, 1950, covers all the basic human rights and the core Labour Standards. In fact a directive principles owe much further on various freedoms. It was pointed out, that "the Indian Constitution was a product of the post war II ear—a seminal period in the development of human rights. Part III also reflects the inspection and the impact of another great chapter of liberties—the Universal Declaration of Human Rights—that was adopted by the United Nations General Assembly in

1948. Many fundamental rights find mention in both the universal declaration and the international covenants. Thus Indian citizens had the good fortune to be constitutionally blessed with many of international covenant's and rights 21 years before Indian became a signatory to it" Table-1 shows the rights that are embodied in both the United Nations constitution and the International Covenant.

Rights Contain in both the Indian Constitution and the International Covenant on United Nations Civil and Political Rights.

Mahatma Gandhi, the great idealist political in India, emphasises the duties form which rights emanate Mahatma Gandhi is very critical (skepticism) about enforceability of United Nations 1948 declaration in the sense of an authority to enforce them. According to Gandhi "The very right to live accrues to us only when we do the duty of citizenship of the world. From this one fundamental statement perhaps it is easy enough to define the duties of man and women and correlate every right to some corresponding duty to be first performed".[6] In fact Gandhi accorded a very high priority to human rights questions. He personally drafted, moved and defended a resolution passed unanimously in 1931 at Karachi session adopted by the Indian National congress. The issues raised by Sen and Gandhi are these deals with the rationals of agencies in ensuring rights. The world can not shy away from them. The United Nation system's attempt in this context are well meaning but lack the authority of the agency to implement it. Mahatma Gandhi, back in 1947, had anticipated these problems of implementation in the absence of a world Government and acceptable international civil authority. However, J.M. Keynes had correctly emphasised the force of ideas when he concluded his powerful book with these words...."It is ideal and ideas alone that rule the world....power of vested interests in grossly aggregated."[7]

Table-1: Rights Contained in both the Indian Constitution and the International Covenant on Civil and Political Rights

International Covenant on Rights	Indian Constitution Fundamental Rights	Name of the Rights: Civil and Political
Article 8(3)	Article 23	Freedom from compulsory labour
Article 14(1)	Article 14	Right to equality
Article 26	Article 15	Protection against discrimination based on any ground
Article 25(c)	Article 16	Right to have access to public service
Article 1(1)and(2)	Article 19(1)(a)	Freedom of Speech
Article 21	Article19(1)(b)	Right to Peaceful Assembly
Article 22(1)	Article 19(1)(c)	Freedom of Association
Article 12(1) and (e)	Article 19(1)(d)	Freedom of Movement and Freedom to choose one's own residence
Article 15(1)	Article 20(1)	Freedom from ex-post factor legislation
Article 14(7)	Article 20(2)	Freedom from double jeopardy
Article (14)(3)(g)	Article 20(3)	Freedom from self incrimination
Article 6(1) and 9(1)	Article21	Right to life personal liberty
Article 9(2)(3) and (4)	Article 22 and 23	Right to legal remedies
Article 18(1)	Article 25	Freedom of thought, religion and conscience
Article 27	Article 29(1)	Rights of minorities

Human rights as an idea, however, has successfully caught the imagination of the humanists and idealists of the world and their anti-culation in international forums, among think tanks and the non-government voluntary organisations within civil societies, have been converging as a major force leading to the emerging paradigm shift.

Specialised agencies of the United Nations in particular ILO, FAO, WTP, UNICEF and in UNDP, have gone to great length in ensuring that human rights move to the core of their respective specialised missions. A higher commissioner for human rights was appointed in 1993 by the United Nations and an office of United Nations High Commission for Human rights was created during 1988-89, Miss Mary Robinson, the High Commissioner has taken on the task of coordinating activities of these agencies pertaining to her portfolio and ensuring that issue of her brief are taken on board.

UNDP[8], consolidated on its earlier reports and studies, has focused on the integration of human rights with sustainable human.

SECTION—III

Structural Adjustment Programme

Structural adjustment is one of the most widely discussed and debated subject among the economists and policy-markers in current years. The subject has been a matter of debate, often controversial, in India during the last decade years since structural reforms programme was initiated in 1991. The labour market issues, often forming part of a larger subject of social dimensions of structural adjustment have also received some attention, but the arguments have often been of a polemical nature primarily because of the lack of objective analysis and investigations. It is for this reason that we have chosen to dwell upon this subject and raise certain issues that may require analysis and informed discussion. Some of the important issues that have arisen as labour market implications of structural adjustment, in general, as well in India, with which intend to deal, are: How far the existing labour market institutions and poultices are compatible with the philosophy and practice of structural adjustment? If they are found to render adjustment difficult, in what direction they need to be reformed? What are the short-term costs of adjustment to labour and how they could be minimised? And what are the short, medium and long-term implications of structural adjustment for employment? These issues are complex in nature and, therefore, are not amenable to definite answers, conclusions and solutions. The propositions made in this presentation could, therefore, at best be treated as tentative, as they are on judgement derived from rather very limited evidence.

Structural Adjustment: Context, Philosophy and Basic Elements

Structural adjustment is an essential part of the process of economic growth and development. In the development literature it has been subsumed in the broader concept of structural change. It primarily implies changing importance and roles of different elements and sectors of the economy in the process of development. It takes place either on the basis of the interplay of market forces of demand and supply, internally and internationally, or is brought about on the basis of conscious and deliberate policy measures adopted mainly on the macro-economic front. Structural adjustment has, however, acquired a narrower and specific meaning in the current international-economic situation. In recent years, particularly since the 1980's, it has been advanced, mainly by the international financial institutions, as a solution to the economic crisis faced by many developing countries on the domestic and external economic fronts. In this specific context, it consists of a set of policy measures particularly aimed at developing countries in debt or otherwise faced with the economic crisis characterised by balance of payment deficits and low rates of economic growth coupled with low rates of interests.

The nature and extent of the problem, its diagnosis and the policy package being implemented may differ among countries, but there is a basic core of propositions common to the structural adjustment programme undertaken in different countries. Balance of payment problems and low rates of inflation and interest rates have been found to be the common of most of these countries. Internal economic instability and high international indebtedness, often leading them to the brink of default in debt servicing have been the immediate reasons to launch the adjustment programme, at the instance of and with the advice and active support from the international financial institutions. The programme has generally consisted of two, closely inter-related, elements; one aiming at stabilisation in terms of sustainable development and restoring balance of payments and the other at structural reforms to lead the national economies on to a higher growth path.

The basic reasons commonly advanced for the economic crisis faced by most countries undergoing structural adjustment are: inward-looking, import-substituting development strategies and high degree of state intervention in and regulation of economic activities by government. High protection of domestic industry that is an inevitable corollary of the import substituting strategy, is supposed to have led to inefficiency and misallocation of investible resources and loss of comparative advantage in international trade. Entry of governments in economic activities which could best be performed by the private sector has resulted in inefficiency and drain on budgetary resources. Regulations of private sector activity has meant unnecessary and undesirable curbs on the operations of economic activity resulting in slower growth of investment, misallocation of investment and encouragement to rent-seeking activities.

In sum, the basic premise of the structural adjustment programmes is that the national economies have not been allowed to function on the basis of the free play of market forces. And, high tariff barriers and over-valued currencies have prevented free flow of goods and services internationally. Macro-economic policies combined with large state intervention and heavy regulation of domestic economic activities have led to severe distortions in the factor and product markets leading to all round inefficiencies, stagnation, and balance of payment crisis. In addition, fiscal profligacy on the part of the governments in public expenditure, particularly in providing for unnecessary and ineffective subsidies and budgetary support to non-performing public enterprises, have resulted in large fiscal deficits, already ignited by slow growth of output. Based on this diagnosis, the philosophy of structural adjustment stresses the urgency to change policies to allow free play of market forces in the domestic and external economic operations and reduce the role of the government to the minimum. Resource allocation and economic outcomes should be left to the market. Macro-economic policies should be geared primarily to monetary stability and control of public expenditure. Government should not only withdraw from all commercial sectors of economic activity and concentrate on preservation of legal framework which facilities smooth functioning of private business, but also remove interventions and regulations that tend to distort the factor and product prices.

Given these basic premises on which the programmes of structural adjustments are based, the package of policy reforms initiated in different countries have included the following measures. On the exchange rate and trade policy front, the measures aim at removing trade barriers and promoting exports. They have consisted of devaluation and establishment of an exchange rate regime more realistically reflecting the value of currencies in the foreign exchange market; and removal of non-tariff restrictions and reduction of tariff rates imports with a view to facilitating freer inflow of essential inputs and products and infusing competition and efficiency in the higher to protected domestic industry. On the fiscal front, the measures include reduction in government expenditure, particularly on subsidies and budgetary support to public enterprises with a view to reducing fiscal deficit. These measures also simultaneously aim in the medium and long run to induce efficiency and reduce misallocation of resources resulting from price distortions that subsidisation has created. Privatisation of public enterprises is another element of the form package aiming simultaneously to reduce government expenditure and, more important, to induce greater efficiency in the operations of these enterprises. On the regulatory front, the major element of the reform package has been to exempt enterprises from the necessity of seeking licenses, permissions and approvals for starting, operating and expanding business operations. Thus liberalisation, privatisation and globalisation (LPG) have became the order of the day.

An Essential Element of Structural Adjustment Labour Market Flexibility

The basic premise of the structural adjustment programmes that the regulation of economic decisions and economic outcomes by government and non-market institutions leads to distortions and results in inefficiency and discourage investment for growth extends to labour market as well. Labour markets, like any other factor and product markets, should be allowed to operate on the basis of the free play of demand and supply forces. It is contended that a high degree of regulation of the labour markets in several countries now undergoing structural adjustment, have resulted not only in inefficient use and high costs of labour but has also discouraged expansion of employment opportunities thus accentuating the problem of unemployment. There are two aspects of the functioning of the labour markets in these countries which have become the targets of frontal attack in the process of structural adjustments: they are, first, the legal provisions and institutions regulating conditions of employment and job security; and second, those rendering wages inflexible in relation to productivity and market conditions. Specific targets of attack are legal provisions protecting job tenure, fixing legally obligatory minimum wage and other quasi-legal process of wage fixation and trade union pressure which is often buttressed by these legal provisions.

Labour market reforms advocated as a part of the structural reform package, therefore, ask for flexibility in the labour market.[9] In concrete form, it would mean relatively complete freedom to enterprises in hiring and firing of workers and determination of wages through the underred play of market forces. These measures are logical corollaries of the philosophy of the structural adjustment which views the enthronement of the market as the vehicle for efficiency and growth. It stands to logic, in this framework, that an enterprise should be free to use only as much labour as it requires for efficient production and dispense with labour when found surplus on efficiency and market considerations. Similarly, and enterprise as a profit maximiser should not be forced to pay a wage in excess of what is warranted by productivity and labour market considerations.

There are, however, several questions that need to be examined in putting this market-led logic to practice. First, there is the moral and social question: whether labour should be treated as a commodity like any other. It has very little scope for consideration in the pure theory of markets. But can it really be ignored? Dealing with labour market we are dealing with human beings and their lives. Wage are, no doubt, a cost to production enterprise, but they are also incomes and most often the sole source of livelihood for a worker. Removing a worker from employment without reasonable notice and without reasonable compensation to survive till he can reasonably be expected to find an alternative source of livelihood and means of survival, or to employ him at wages below subsistence level, even though dictated by the market may, therefore, not be socially acceptable. That is the reason why certain safeguards and standards have been internationally accepted in relation to employment conditions and minimum wages and it would be retrograde to completely bid a good-bye to them for the reasons of economic and technical efficiency judged primarily on the criterion of private profit.

But even on a economic basis, there are at least two questions that need to be asked: first, whether job insecurity and low and uncertain wages lead to higher efficiency and productivity than employment with a minimum job security and minimum assured wages, and second, whether job security provisions and minimum wage legislation tend to discourage employment growth, as is argued by the proponents of labour market flexibility. On the face of it, it seems quite logical to assume that flexible wage system and freedom to adjust workforce and essential conditions for efficient production. At the same time, however, there is large body of theoretical literature on 'efficiency of high and assured wages, and positive effects of job security on commitment and productivity of workers. Similarly, it is true that job security regulations requiring government permission and union acceptance for lay-off and retrenchment and mandated high severance wages, raise the direct and transaction costs of reduction of staff. But it does not necessarily follow that such provisions lead to a smaller volume of employment. For an enterprises, to carry out expansion in production without expanding employment, certain technological and economic conditions need to be satisfied. First a choice of techniques to facilitate substitution between labour and capital should be physically available to the producer to decide in favour of a less labour-using technology of production. Second, such technology should be equally, if not more, efficient than the labour-using technology already in practice. it is well known that choices of techniques allowing wide range of substitutions between labour and capital are generally not available. Many economists, therefore, believe that most often choices are only among products and not among techniques to produce the same product.

Some Basic Facts of the Theory of Labour Market Flexibility

At a more general level, the proposition that labour market rigidities caused by government regulations of wages and job tensures restrict expansion of employment opportunities and create unemployment has its origin in the neo-classical concept of 'market clearing'. Market clearing implies elimination of shortages and surpluses by directing demands and supplies through flexible prices. Such clearing is supposed to take place more efficiently in unregulated markets. Specifically in the labour market, it would imply that if wages are left to be completely freely determined by the demand and supply situation and no institutional restraints are placed on the hiring and firing of labour, the labour market would eventually clear: all labour will be employed and unemployment would disappear. It is well known that while demand for labour may respond to wages, this response is never unlimited: it is conditioned by investments and technology because demand for labour is a derived demand. Elasticity of labour supply, with respect to wages, is of course, much more erratic and uncertain, due to such exogenous factors like the growth of population and labour force and human mobility.

Even the most orthodox among the economists would, therefore, easily accept that labour markets do not necessarily clear; persistence of unemployment is not an uncommon phenomenon. Also, labour markets everywhere are segmented; and, wage-differentials unrelated to efficiency, productivity and relative demand-supply situation in the occupational labour markets, are the rule rather than exceptions and, quite often, casual, unstable and low paid employment even the most orthodox among the economists would, therefore, easily accept that labour markets do not necessarily clear; persistence of unemployment is not an uncommon phenomenon. Also, labour markets everywhere are segmented; and, wage-differentials unrelated to efficiency, productivity and relative demand-supply situation in the occupational labour marks, are the rule rather than exceptions and, quite often, casual, unstable and low paid employment exists alongside high paid protected job. It would be native to attribute these phenomena, which present a contrast to the neo-classical concept of neat an orderly labour market capable to clearing, to the legal and policy interventions by the governments and unions. These phenomena exist in all labour markets, regulated or unregulated; they may vary in degree but not in essence. The neo-classical economic theory is, of course, versatile enough to view these phenomena as 'aberrations' and results of the limitations of imperfect information and to insist that the labour markets would clear and wage-differentials would only relate to productivity differentials, if information were freely available. The fact, however, remains that since information is not a free good, and labour supply and mobility is not a function solely of the wage rate, the concept of labour market clearing remains a myth.

Labour market clearing is thus unconvincing even as an abstract theoretical hypothesis. But it needs to be more closely examined if important economic and social policy measures are sought to be derived as an implication of this hypothesis. In the context of structural adjustment, the advocacy of labour market flexibility largely rests on this theoretical hypothesis, "Labour market clearing" in the new-classical sense refers to the process through which the labour market arrives at a situation in which there is no involuntary unemployment. Existence and persistence of unemployment, therefore, implies absence of this process cause by legal and institutional regulation of wages and employment; and, labour market would be cleared of involuntary unemployment if such regulations are removed and labour is permitted to be used in a flexible manner and at a wage that truly reflects its relative price, relative to the demand-supply situation in the labour market as well as to the price of capital. We have already drawn attention to the fallacies of assumptions underlying the theoretical construct of this hypothesis. it has great practical significance for the proper development of core labour standards and the human rights.

SECTION—IV

Core Labour Standards and Human Rights in India

The structural change in terms of changes in the institutional arrangements at the national and global level have come to occupy crucial prominence since the early 1980s in the name of economic reforms with its components of stabilisation and Structural Adjustment Programme. while stabilisation programme is used to describe the short run methods aimed at correcting the fiscal deficits and keeping a control on prices. Structural Adjustment Programme is devised as a medium terms programme, which aims at the progressive diminishing role of the states in the economy by deregulation, disinvestment and privatisation. The Structural Adjustment programme, may be seen as consisting of many components with specific reference to developing countries.

The retreat of the state from the commanding heights and thus from the prime role of mobilier and investor of resources. In the India context since the attainment of independence and adoption of planning as an instrument of economic development the state has surveyed as the leading actor of eco-development. But the shifts in the structure of the economy and the adoption of Structural Adjustment Programme challenged the planned development strategies. Further, emphasis on private sector under Structural Adjustment Programme reduced the state to the status of a disinvestor and nobody knows much about the 10th Five year plan which is due to commence from April 2002. The seasonal dimension of the Structural Adjustment Programme involves a shift in emphasis from the production of capital goals to consumer goods under the guise of flow of resources, appropriateness of skills and technology for increasing efficiency.

The most important component of the Structural Adjustment Programme in the liberalisation of internal and international trade to facilitate free movement of not only goods and services but also capital. It is on this aspect of the Structural Adjustment programme some used the description of gloablisation. Surprisingly, globalisation is often used synonymously with Structural Adjustment Programme. The Structural Adjustment programme which entails withdrawal of the State from the economy, is a direct product of the 'Counter Revolution' in the development thinking. These views on counter revolution had become the ideological basis for the Structural Adjustment Programme anyway. With respect to labour markets in it shown that Structural Adjustment programme requires or more flexible labour markets.[10] This implies.

(a) flexibility of real wages in the organised industry.

(b) form hiring to firing of labour

(c) the adoption of free exist policy by firms including the public sector, which is under pressure to down size.

The implications of Structural Adjustment Programme on Core Labour Standards are far reaching. An interesting study by some economists on union function and employment and such other related issues amply demonstrated the adverse effects of Structural Adjustment programme.[11] Besides fiscal contractions, privatisation of public sector and removal of cross border economic barriers, Structural Adjustment programme with its compulsions of fierce competition has brought about drastic changes in the industrial organisation and management with severe consequences on the livelihood of the working class and fundamental human rights. In the developed countries globalisation seems to be an important course of job losses as corporations downsize their employment in the face of cut throat competition. The rising wage, income inequality, unemployment that occurred in a number of countries are associated with globalisation (ILO). Referring to cross country experiences of the Structural Adjustment programme the human development report 1996 summarises 'the market driven growth as jobless, ruthless, voiceless, restless and futureless'. It drives have the fact that Structural Adjustment programme has let loose a process of casualising and information, which is causing dislocation of communities by minimising employment opportunities and reducing employment in the organised sector and increasing the mass of working poor. In India the prospects of employment growth in the organised sector are bleak and its informalisation may render the labour organisation weak. With the unfolding of the consequences of Structural Adjustment programme undermined the position of labour as a factor of production. This is likely to worsen with the privatisation of public sector, the growing trend of contracting out formal sector jobs to informal sector and the introduction of informal labour practices into the formal sector. The examples reported here are by far only a few of the several initiatives to ensure fuller and purposeful to the working population by enjoying core Labour Standards and basic Human Rights. In the face of the treat of growing dislocation and uncertainty that are inherent in the immerging structural changes and also in the context of the demand for the second generation economic reforms in India in recent years draws attention to the new initiatives in organising labour in India.

The above discussion shows that Labour Standards ratified so far are not adequate to help India face up to the challenge of structural adjustments. This judgment would hold even when one includes the provision of National Renewal Fund (NRF) to complement the Labour Standards, the enormity of the challenge would be all the greater if they are linked with core Labour Standards or to trade materials. Any attempt by the WTO to overstep the legitimate boundaries of trade and cross the jurisdiction of domestic production system is bour to create serious problems and raise basic question about WTO's competence and credibility. This calls for trade union transformation in adopting social movement, unionism and the scope for organizing the unorganised informal sector workers and peasant worker alliance. The case in this direction is a National Campaign Committee for rural worker (NCCRW) set up some five years age. It comprises most of the major national trade union centres and also a large number of rural activists group as participants. The idea behind the formation of NCCRW was that the organised trade union movement should form an integral movement of the entire masses of working people in the country.[12] Further, the Structural Adjustment programme influence the industrial relation system in India and created a new regional pattern of industrial relations. Decentralised union, now organisational structures has emerged in some parts of rural India with the initiative for voluntary organisations.[13]

SECTION—V

Vision for 21st Century

Core Labour Standards adopted by the member countries of International Labour Organisation have amply demonstrated the real value of these standards to improve the quality of life, efficiency and productivity under global conditions. These standards can help to deepen the understanding and broaden the usefulness of human rights approach. Similarly human rights approach may offer an additional and very useful perspective for the analysis of Core Labour Standards and Human Development. Finally, a close relationship can be established between core labour standards and human rights analysis. The levels of economic development will provide the base line to establish the relations between these two. Such analysis can enrich our assessment of social problem by helping us to become more attuned to future of a society that might not be adequately emphasized in human development accounting.

At the dawn of the 21st century the United Nations has become more central to the lies of more people than ever. The Secretary General of United Nations pointed our, "Intervention, however, is not just a matter for states. Each one of us whatever a worker in government, in inter governmental or non-governmental organisations, in business, in the media, or simply as a human being has an obligation to do whatever he or she can to define the human rights of our fellow men and women when they are threatened. Each of us has a duty to halt or, better to prevent he infliction of suffering"[14]. Defining the comparative advantage of different institutions is the starting point of implementation strategy. Many institutions have multiple and overlapping roles. but each has a comparative advantage and concentrating on strengths those can increases their effectiveness particular when partnerships recognise that other institutions are focusing other elements of advocacy and implementation. The 21st century should be the century, for the world wide spread of freedom. all people have the right to enjoy seven freedoms and core labour standards. Each of these standards and rights requires a vision worthy of collective effort by the nations of the world. Strengthening of labour institutions, core labour standards and acceptance of basic human rights will provide foundation's for protecting or safeguarding the on slaught of globalisation. Thus the university of basic human rights, core labour standards provides the foundation for global vision.

The global going in democracy are still very recent. The 21st century should give all people for the first time in the history—the right to choose their government and the freedom to participate in the decision that affect their lives. An active involvement in civic institutions and unprecedented access to information and knowledge will enhance the foundation of global vision. What is unique to the 21st century is a commitment to work for the abolition of oppressive working conditions. There are ambitious goals. Yet there is nothing new in these aspirations. But the uniqueness of the 21st century is the possibility that those aspirations can become a reality for all people. The protect movement against the effects of globalisation emerged in several places around the world which strengthened the struggle for just labour standards, real human rights in the frame work of structural adjustment programme.

REFERENCES

1. Sengen Berger Werner "Labour Standards", and Institutional Frame Work for Restructuring and Development in Sengen Berger, Werner and Duncan Campbell (editor), Growing Economic Opportunities: The Role of Labour Standards in Industrial Restructuring, International Institute for Labour Studies, 1994, Geneva.

2. Castle, R.G., D.P. Chaudhary, et.al. Labour Clauses, the World Trade Organisation and Child Labour in India, The Indian Journal of Labour Economics, 1997, January-March.

3. D.P. Chaudhary. "Basic Human Rights, Core Labour Standards and Relative Deprivation of Youth in India". The Indian Journal of Labour Economics, January-March 2001, pp. 44-45.

4. Prof. A.K. Sen Provides a cogent summary of the position. Sen has presented the link between capabilities and entitlement as well as the community effects, particularly in the context of gender bias in his writings. Some of them are:

   (a) Prof. A.K. Sen, Liberty, Unanimity and Rights, 1982.

   (b) Development as Freedom, Oxford 1999.

   (c) Prof. A.K. Sen, The Possibility of Social Choice, Noble Lecture Reprinted in the American Economic Review, 1999. Volume 89 No. (3).

5. "Eastern Strategy: a Plan for Asia's Growth", Second Asia Pacific Lecture, Singapore, July 1999, as reported in Asia Work, October, 8, pp. 62-63.

6. A.K. Das Gupta, Gandhi's Economic Thought, Routledge, London, 1996, p. 42.

7. J.M. Keynes, The General Theory of Money Employment and Interest, Mc. Millon, London, 1936.

8. UNDP Integrating Human Rights with Sustainable Development, 1998, New York, p. 6.

9. An excellent summary on SAP and Employment and waged was provided by Prof.. T.S. Papolai in presidential address to the Annual Conference of the Indian. Society of Labour Economics on "SAP Labour market, Flexibility and Employment" Gandhi Labour Institute, January 21-23, 1994, Ahmedabad In fact I borrowed very liberally from this address on SAP.

10. Baduri, A, "Employment Labour/Market Flexibility and Economic Liberalisation in India". The Indian Journal of Labour Economics, 1996, Vol. 1.39, 1.

11. Reddy, D.N. "Structural Change, Structural Adjustment and Challenges to Unions" India Journal of Labour Economic, Vol. 43, No. 2, April-June 2000. pp. 203-221.

12. Tulpule, B., "Trade unions on the Threshold of 21st Century", paper presented at the Seminar on Trade Union

Movement on the threshold of 21st Century, Sharmika Prathistana, Mumbai, August, 1999.

13. Chandra, N., and Reddy, D.N., "Voluntary action and Rural Labour Markets in India" in Radhakrishna R. and Alak N. Sharma (editors). Empowering Rural Labour in India, Mumbai, August 1-2, 1999.

14. Kofi Annan "Human Development Report" 2000. UNDP, Oxford University Press, 2000, p. 31.

9

Institutional Labour Standards on Human Rights—A Review

Dr. K. Uma Devi

Global concern for human rights is of recent origin, though some few principles of humanitarian intervention were institutionalized by the League of Nations in 1918. The U.N. Charter provides the foundation for a global approach to human rights:

> ... to reaffirm faith in fundamental human rights, in the dignity and worth of the human person, in the equal rights of men and women of all nations, large and small.

Article I of the U.N. Charter contains that:

> ... to achieve international co-operation in solving international problems of economic, social, cultural, or humanitarian character, and in promoting and encouraging respect for human rights and for fundamental freedoms for all without distinction as to peace, sex, language, or religion.

The United Nations lost no time in dealing with human rights and it proclaimed a Universal Declaration of Human Rights in 1948. Several Articles of UDHR cover a wide range of basic human rights and fund mental freedoms as developed in the Western World. In addition to the initiatives taken by the U.N. General Assembly, several other international organisations have made important contributions to human rights standards. The European Convention on Human Rights and affiliated protocols have established workable procedures and precedents. The United Nations Educational, Scientific and Cultural Organisation has instituted conventions against discrimination in education. The International Labour Organisation adopted a number of conventions and recommendations for setting international labour standards including the right to organise and bargain, the abolition of slavery, and the establishment of equal remuneration for equal work. In this paper an attempt has been made to review and examine the international labour standards on human rights.

UDHR and Labour Standards

Article 23:

(i) Everyone has the right to work, free choice of employment, just and favourable conditions of work and protection against unemployment;

(ii) Everyone who works has the right to just and equitable remuneration ensuring for himself and his family an existence worthy of human dignity, and supplemented, if necessary, by other means of social protection;

(iii) Everyone has the right to fight and to join trade unions for the protection of him.

Article 24: Every one has the right to rest and leisure including reasonable limitation of working hours and periodic holidays with pay.

Article 7: of the International Covenant on Economic, Social and Cultural Rights emphasizes:

(i) Fair wage and equal remuneration for work of equal value without discrimination of any kind in

general and women in particular, being guaranteed conditions of work not inferior to those enjoyed by men, and with equal pay for equal work

(ii) **(a)** decent living for themselves and their families in accordance with the provisions of the present Covenant;

(b) safe and healthy conditions of work;

(c) equal opportunity for every to be promoted in his employment to an appropriate higher level subject to no considerations other than those of seniority and competence;

(d) Rest, leisure and reasonable limitation of working hours and periodic holidays worth pay as well as remuneration for public holidays.

Hence, labour has become an important component in evolving international Human Rights.

I.L.O. and Labour Standards on Human Rights

International Labour Organisation was established in 1919 as a part of the League of Nations. It was intended to serve the aims of international peace through the establishment of social justice. Setting of International Labour Standards as well as their observance in association with workers' and employers organisations and the government of member countries are amongst the primary activities of the I.L.O. The prime motive behind this is to establish social justice, human conditions of work, social security and quality of life for the working class within the overall framework of human rights and freedom of association. The International Labour Standards set by the ILO have been instrumental in ameliorating the lost of workers throughout the world and in ensuring better standards of living and conditions of work for them. These standards have greatly influenced labour and social legislations in India, as elsewhere in the world. India has so fare ratified 35 International Labour Standards out of 172 adopted by ILO. International labour standards endeavour to help member countries develop socially and economically in a manner conducive to the promotion of social justice and improvement of quality of life of the working people. With a view to enhancing national capabilities in the matter of standards, ILO has not only been expanding the area of technical cooperation but also innovating in the mode of action. ILO's assistance include the supply of documentation, technical advice, experts' services and consultancy and financial support.

Overview of ILS with Emphasis on Human Rights Conventions

A large number of ILO standards (conventions and Recommendations) addressed to a variety of subjects such as basic human rights, social security, safety and health, etc. While Convention No. 87 on freedom of association, applied to all categories of employees, there were others which applied only specific sectors of economic activities. Basic human rights Conventions were thus much wider in scope and there were three sub-categories of such Conventions:

> ..... freedom of association, prohibition of forced labour, and equality of treatment. The category of prohibition of forced labour Conventions comprised two Conventions, No. 29 and 105; the first one has been ratified by nearly 130 countries. Convention No. 105 slightly differed from Convention No. 29 as it enumerated five types of cases which were considered forced labour, thereby widening the scope; thus prison labour could also be considered one type of forced labour.

The Convention on non-discrimination (No. 111) covered several types of discrimination, the Convention on Equal remuneration (No. 100) related only to payment of wages. The Convention on freedom of association (No. 87) guaranteed freedom from public interference in unionisation in any manner and at any level, whereas Convention No.

98 on collective bargaining referred to the relationship between the employer and employees. Both convention Nos. 87 and 98 allowed police and armed forces to be covered by other arrangements. Unlike Convention No. 87 which covered all employments, Convention No. 98 exempted public servants in the administration of the state. AS Convention No. 87 referred only to an industrial organisation and not a political organisation, it was not likely to present any difficulty in regard to public servants in India who had no such freedom now. As regards the question of flexibility in ILO standards, there is good deal of flexibility with general labour standards but such flexibility could not be introduced in human rights Conventions.

The other human rights conventions are:

(i) Convention No. 127 concerning Maximum Weight, 1967:

It was unanimously agreed that a time had come when serious efforts should be made to prescribe the maximum permissible weight to be carried by a worker. It was agreed that the main areas of concern was packing of foodgrains and sugar which continued to be packed in 100 kg. bags. Considering the importance of the Convention from the point of safety, health and welfare, it was recommended that the maximum weight should be 50 kg. net packing in respect of foodgrains and sugar.

(ii) Convention No. 139 concerning occupational Cancer, 1974. It was strongly felt that this was an area where certain positive steps ought to be taken urgently to minimise, if not eliminate, the risk of exposure to carnicnogenic substances, both in the organised and unorganised sectors.

(iii) Convention No. 155 concerning Occupational Safety and Health and the working Environment, 1981.

It was an umbrella type of Convention with the basic objective of laying down a national policy on occupational safety and health which would be applicable to all work places in all branches of economic activity.

(*iv*) Convention No. 138 concerning Minimum Age 1973.

It suggested to prescribe the minimum age below which a child could not be employed in any work place. Accordingly the Child Labour (Prohibition and Regulation) Act, 1980 and the National Policy on Child Labour, 1987 were adopted by India.

(*v*) Convention No. 99, concerning Minimum wage fixing Machinery (Agriculture), 1951.

It was felt that the minimum wages should not be less than the poverty line. Accordingly Central government suggested Rs. 20 as the statutory minimum wage with an element of variable dearness allowance.

(*vi*) Convention No. 102: concerning Social Security, 1952.

It was noted that the Convention provided for nine main branches of Social Security, namely, medical care, sickness benefit, employment injury benefit, maternity benefit, unemployment benefit, old age benefit, invalidity benefit, family benefit and survivors' benefit. Further, the Convention laid down a prescribed percentage of coverage of the prescribed classes of employees, or economically active population or residents.

(*vii*) Convention No. 103 concerning Maternity protection, 1952.

Though the existing laws in the country significantly met the equipments of this Convention it would be ratified immediately since it felt short of the provisions relating to the coverage of women employed in industrial undertakings and in non-industrial and agricultural occupations, including women wage earners at home. The world often forget the purpose for which these standards are set. World countries often forget that the prime motive for those who framed the ILO constitution—as an integral part of the 1919. Peace Treaty—was to seek and establish social justice as an essential factor for maintenance of a universal and lasting peace. But the objective has not yet been achieved. Conditions of labour involving injustice, hardship and privation still persist in most parts of our planet and particularly so in developing regions. Each member state which joins the ILO and accepts its constitution, accepts also the obligations et therein. These obligations include the observance and respect of the labour standards particularly those which are considered Basic Human Rights Standards. But majority of the member countries failed to observe and respect these standards.

At the End...

India has sponsored restructuring of its national economy and industrial structure on a big scale in view of the emerging progressive globalisation of economic activity, narrowing of ideological ranks, and liberalisation of economic and financial systems. The ILO itself had aimed at, and worked for such a new world economic order since mid-seventies, with sectoral/regional coordination through technical cooperation programmes so as to ensure step by step linkage in human resources development at the optimum level, and for securing generally universalised labour standards on human rights. This, undoubtedly, has been an uphill task involving tenacity, patience and cultivation of a sense of conviction and farsightedness in the approach of the ground forces of the social partners.

India plunged into economic reforms in hasty without any conviction and far-sightedness. It jumped to integrated world economy without any checks and control. No regulations were imposed on foreign free trade. As a result globalisation is creating new inequities and new challenges, as the Human Development Report 1998 explains. The grave disparity in conditions of life is aggravated with each passing day and an explosive escalation is close upon us worldwide since massive suppression of human rights may will blow up the unjust systems. The vast majority of mankind, inhumanly denied the basic opportunity for survival in dignity, decency and holistic development. In the light of globalisation, liberalisation and privatisation, a drastic changes have been proposed in the labour standards which are detrimental to the Indian labour. The human rights crisis is climaxing and they remain meaningless in the present situation. To quote Napolean Bonaparte:

"There is only one thing in this world, and that is to keep acquiring money and more money, power and more power. All the rest is meaningless".

REFERENCES

1. Bani Borgohain, *Human Rights, Social Justice and Political Challenge*, Kanishka Publishers, Distributors, New Delhi, 1999.
2. Human Rights, 2001, Vigil India Movement.
3. International Labour Standards, National Labour Institute, 1993.
4. Subramanya, R.K.A. "Social Aspects of Structural Adjustment in India", Friedrich Ebert Shiftung, 1996.
5. Verma, S.K. and Kusum, Editors, *Fifty Years of the Supreme Court of India. Its Grasp and Reach*, Indian Law Institute, Oxfort Press, New Delhi, 2001.

10

New Industrial Labour—Insecure Employment, Social Conflict and Labour Rights

G.Vijay

SECTION—I

Introduction

Industrial relations seem to be undergoing drastic changes in the recent times. The relationship between the employers and employees in the industries for long was guided by certain legal provisions. However, in the recent past, many changes in the policies have deregulated the formal sector. The result in that we have the emergence of what are called New Industries. "*New industrialisation* refers to the industrialisation in the changed structure of the economy. Especially industrialisation that is least regulated. New industrialisation also implies industries being situated in newtownships, adapting new technologies and new modes of organising production especially in the sense that there are new methods of organising work and workers" (G. Vijay, 1999). New Industrial Labour markets have come to be flexible. Originally, *flexibility* has been defined as "a strategy of permanent innovation: accommodation to ceaseless change, rather than an effort to control it. This strategy is based on flexible-multi-use equipment; skilled workers; and the creation through the politics of an industrial community that restricts the forms of competition to those favouring innovation". (Piore and Sable, 1984). Further, "in flexible specialisation, product characteristic is the key component of the competitive strategy. It involves greater product variety, with variation within product, greater quality of product and product innovation. The production has to react to fast changes in the market. The output is in small batches of customised products (collectively output may be large). The production is not standardised. The same machine can make a number of products (multi-purpose machines), depending on demand. Greater flexibility of output requires changes in the work practices, and requires multi-tasking and multi-skilling of workforces. They are broadly trained and are required to have conception of work. The main strength lies on continuous innovation with knowledgeable workers. New flexible technologies allow a greater range of output. The factory layouts are altered from dedicated lines and functional layout to flexible production cells. Relationship with other firms becomes organic, which promote innovation and flexible just-in-time production, they are not required to maintain inventory. This is in contrast to mass production which requires to maintain buffer just-in-case anything goes wrong (Piore and Sable, 1984 in Subesh K. Das and P. Panayiotopoulos, 1996). In this sense, flexibility meant that workers specialised in different skills and could handle several activities simultaneously. And technology was such that more than one product could be produced with it. However, flexibility in labour surplus economies like India have come to connote a different meaning. Simply put flexibility in these countries implies to be able to change the labour market rules with the changes in the market, i.e., to be able to hire and fire workers when production increases and decreases, to be able to increase and decrease wages when the demand for workers increases and decreases and so on. Such a method in the new-industries leaves workers disorganised and turns identities into weapons of conflict for resources. The new industrial model is not only an outcome of the new policy, which is making agriculture less remunerative, but is also an outcome of the great environmental catastrophe this development model has left. Many parts of the country do not have normal rainfall. Tis could be an outcome of plethora of reasons but certainly the bore-well technology has had a devastating impact on the water table sometimes driving regions into desensitisation. The urban-industry biased policies and the environmental reasons have pushed people out of the rural areas. And sociai networks, coincidences, and opportunities have attracted people into the industrial towns such as kothur. Kothur is a new industrial township located in Mahaboobnagar district, thirty kilometres to the south-west of Hyderbad, capital of Andhra Pradesh. The district of Mahaboobnagar is well known for its *Palamoor* labour, with the dubious distinction of witnessing the highest seasonal migration in the country of over one million annually to different parts of the country. Paradoxically, the industrialised areas of the district witness massive inflow of migrant labour from different parts of the country. This paradox poses a challenge to research. The total population of the township itself is over ten thousand, however, workers are also settled in the adjacent villages, Kothur is the most industrialised township of Mahaboobnagar district. In this backdrop, the new industries turns modern industrial labour markets into a continuum of rural labour markets. The workers compete being in a state of material insecurity and cultural chaos. Yet it needs to be asserted that even in this insecure socio-economic context, workers forge bonds of solidarity. These bonds are forged sometimes to survive and sometimes motivated by finer human sentiments. The reductionist notions of economic development—where development is growth, (whether be it through an 'open economy' or through the 'nationalist accumulation') have not solved human problems. It will not be far from truth to say that growth does not have solutions to the complex social problems that the world is faced with. It can even be asserted that growth which is driven by competitive markets may far from solving the fundamental conflicts may end up complicating the social context. To make all social institutions an arena of competition so as to be able to derive efficiency, seems to make efficiency a finality, an intrinsic purpose, and a philosophy in itself even when devoid of any positive social outcome. Growth as being pursued by the economic reforms displaces people, pushing them to move out of their old social niches, into a situation where human beings coexist with a mutual perception of rivalry and all social relations are slowly reduced to a 'means' underlying which is an instrumentalist philosophy with a clear material purpose, such a development process can lead to collapse of social cohesion by systematically destroying social institutions leaving deep social crisis. This paper tries to focus on this growing social crisis and how markets affect labour rights. This tries to answer the following questions:

1. What are the trends in labour markets in the changed context of development?
2. What is the worst case scenario of employment?
3. What is the social crisis which present development model creates?
4. Are there any institutions capable of addressing the social crisis?

The paper is divided into five sections. The second section deals with the overall trends in the labour market, the third section presents empirical findings of the worst case scenario in the labour markets, the fourth section presents case studies which reflect the social crisis and the crisis of labour rights which new industrial model creates, the fifth section presents some institutions which are dealing with the social crisis and the question of labour rights.

SECTION—II

Uncertain Formal Employment as a Growing Phenomena

It is argued that "for many years informal employment, although its existence was not denied, was assumed to be in decline and/or of little relevance for understanding and interpreting advanced economies and their prospects. Instead, an assumption prevailed that informal employment was a mere leftover from a previous era of production. Work and welfare would become increasingly formalised and result in an end-state of full employment and comprehensive and universal formal welfare provision. However, the history of the past twenty years in advanced economies and beyond has taught us that such as assumption can no longer be accepted" (Colin. C. Williams and Jan Windebank, 1998: 5).

It was asserted long ago that "when they arrived in the cities, however, migrants encountered a hostile world...the migrants discovered that their numbers were considerable, that the system was not prepared to accept them, that more and more barriers were being erected against them, that they had to fight to extract every right from an unwilling establishment, that they were excluded from the facilities and benefits offered by the law, and that ultimately, the only guarantee of their freedom and prosperity lay in their own hands. In short, they discovered that they must compete not only against people but also against the system... thus it was, that in order to survive, the migrants became informals" (Hemando de Soto, 1989). Informal in this sense of use is almost concomitant with illegal (also see: Saskia Sasser, 1997; Victor, E. Tokman, 1992). This conception of informality is very limited. In the recent past, the legal and political barriers to the entry of informal workers into the erstwhile formal sector are being gradually removed. The formal sector has been gradually deregualted and the trajectory suggests that over the period the distinction between formal and informal may be dubious. When the migrants entered the 'formal' sector, far from their employment being formalised, those who had formal employment seem to be loosing it. A recent statement by the Finance Minister of India puts the new policy perspective:

The only distinction that still remains between formal and informal is the minimum wage regulation and some protections like ESI and PF. In practice even these are often overlooked by the regulatory bodies or officials. This change from formal to informal has been described as *information* (Colin. C. Williams and Jan Windebank, 1998). And it has been argued that information is a 'form of advanced capitalist exploitation' (Chew, Denemark, 1996). This however captures only one part of the overall change. Since the process is not just one of deregulating the formal sector, but it is one of legitimising what would have earlier been 'illegal'. A more pertinent understanding of 'informal' is "for most part, unregistered, operating on a very small scale and with a low level of organisation. Most of them have very low levels of productivity and income. They tend to have little or no access to organised markets, to credit institutions, to modern technology, to formal education and training facilities, and to many public services and amenities. A large number of them are carried on without any fixed location, or in places that are not visible to the authorities, such as small (work) shops or residences. They are not recognised, supported or regulated by the government and are often compelled by circumstances to operate outside the framework of the law. Even where they are registered and respect certain aspects of the law, they are almost invariably beyond the bound of social protection, labour legislation and protective measures at the workpalce" (Ralf Hussmanns, 1996). However, the new

Finance Minister's Budget Speech 2001-02

"It is also necessary to address the contentious issue of rigidities in our labour legislation. Some existing provisions in the Industrial Disputes Act have made it almost impossible for industrial firms to exercise any labour flexibility. The Government is now convinced that some change is necessary in this legislation. Chapter VB of the ID Act stipulates that employers in specified industrial establishments must obtain prior approval of the appropriate government authority for effecting lay-off, retrenchment and closure, after following the prescribed procedure. It is proposed that these provisions may now apply to industrial establishment employing not less than 1000 workers instead of 100, the separation compensation will be increased from 15 days to 45 days for every completed year of service. The enhancement of compensation would act as a deterrent on employers to take recourse to lay-off, retrenchment and closure in a routine manner.

Similarly, rigities inherent in the existing legislation regarding Contact Labour inhibit growth in employment in many service activities. Section 10 of the existing Act envisages prohibition of contract labour in work/process/operation if the conditions set therein like perennial nature of job etc. are fulfilled. Section 10 enables the contract labour engaged in prohibited jobs to become direct employees of the principal employer. To overcome this difficulty and at the same time ensure the protection of labour, it is proposed to being an amendment to facilitate outsourcing of activities without any restrictions as well as to offer contract appointments. It would not differentiate between core and non-core activities, and provide protection to labour engaged in outsourced activities in terms of their health, safety, welfare, social security, etc. It would also provide for larger compensation based on last drawn wages as retrenchment compensation for every year of service.

These measures will promote industrial investment in labour intensive, and export oriented activities providing for renewed industrial growth, while, at the same time safeguarding the interest of workers. My colleague, the Minister for Labour, will introduce appropriate legislation to amend the Industrial Disputes act and Contract Labour Act within this session."

Source: http://exim.indiamart.com/budget-2001-02/speech/budget-drug-price-control.html#labor-market.

industrialisation has many distinct features from the indicators associated with the informal sector. Firstly, the relatively less regulated labour markets of new industries can be associated with "unregistered" only in so far as some small scale industries are concerned while informal employment exists in large and medium scale industries and well. "Low level of organisation" is true but the phenomenon of company unions have rendered unions without role. "Very low levels of productivity and income" is not true. Productivity is quite high for example in industries such as Hyderabad Industries Ltd. which has a total investment of rs. 8 corers and employs only fifteen workers, of which 11 are informal workers. Ideas that "they ten dot have little or no access to organised markets" or "a large number of them are carried on without any fixed location, or in places that are not visible to the authorities, such as small (work) shops or residences" or "They are not recognised, supported or regulated by the government and are often compelled by circumstances to operate outside the framework of the law" is a travesty as all these manufacturing industries themselves fall under organised industry and enjoy many benefits of government's incentive packages. "Lack of access to credit institutions, to modern technology, to formal education and training facilities, and to many public services and amenities" is completely true. The observation that "even where they are registered and respect certain aspects of the law, they are almost invariably beyond the bound of social protection, labour legislation and protective measures at the workpalce" is also true. This divergence is an outcome of a process which is not merely one of informalising employment but one of informalising laws and rules of the labour market. It is not a flexibility of the labour market but flexibility of laws and rules of the labour market. Since these forms of employment existed even earlier, flexibility of employment existed even when the so called regid rules were in place. What has happened now is that State has become more flexible. It has acknowledged and accommodated the flexible employment patterns. When the state endorses flexible employment, the only other source of resistance comes from labour organisations. This the managements of different industries are doing away with, by recruiting migrants in place of the locals workers. Migration as a phenomenon not only bring better opportunities for those migranting, but while migranting, the migrants carry with them their *vulnerability*" not the places of destination. Migration is no longer a process of bringing in skilled labour but it is a method of vulnerablising the labour markets. What the new policy does by deregulating is, it allows the labour as a collective to become vulnerable. The new pattern of employment is therefore not merely one of informalisation but one of *Vulnerabilisation*". The vulnerable labour markets are in-turn generating an insecure workforce (Edmund Heery and John Salmon, 2000). Where workers have no protections against the vagaries of the market.

SECTION—III

Flexibilisation of Erratic Oscillation?

"Marketisation and privatisation engender another, more automatic economic and social polarisation of income and position, also between the genders, and among class and ethnic groups and regions. A minority will float to the surface of a first ebbing and then rising tide, and the majority will be sunk even farther below the surface" (A.G. Frank, 1996-39). What will happen to those that sink below is narrated by the stories of workers from a new industrial town called Kothur. What have flexible labour market practices done is they have generated lot of uncertainty for the workers. They have created what may be termed as an erratic oscillation in the lives of workers. Workers economic, social, political and cultural space is filled with unpredictability. Most certainly what workers treasured the most in formal employment—Stability is lost to the competitive markets. What follows is a narration of some forms of such an Erratic Oscillation:

1. **Oscillation Across Time:** If time is divided into some basic units such as days, weeks, seasons, or years with reference to employment, modes of payment, treatment of experience etc., there is a discursive mobility and in this sense it reflects oscillation. Following case studies can establish the point:

> Uma Devi (28) is a migrant from Shadnagar. She has come here after her family suffered a loss in Kirana shop[1] business because of moral hazards in credit sales. Every day she wakes up at 3:30 a.m. and cooks for the family, takes a tiffin box for herself and reaches factory by 5:15 a.m. If she finds work for the day, she comes back home after 12 hours of work by 6:30 p.m. Till 9.30 p.m. she has the duties of shopping, cleaning the house, washing clothes, cleaning utensils, and of-course cooking. She goes to bed at 10 p.m. Early in the morning she undergoes tremendous tension because she has to reach the industry before the ceremony of punching the cards by which they are recruited is over. For workers like Uma Devi, every day is an uncertain day.

The oscillation is also across seasons. Following case study will throw light on this aspect:

> R.B. Yadav (28) is a long distant migrant from Bihar. He is employed as a casual worker in a textile industry which does printing on cotton cloth. There are cycles in operation which the company undergoes. In rainy seasons, the company is closed because the printed cloth cannot be soaked in the sun. the company has a peak production period during festival seasons, when the demand for clothes goes up. In the beginning of the rainy season when we reached to interview Yadav, he was a sad man. During the rainy season workers are laid-off and re-recruited as soon as it is over.

2. **Oscillation Across Regions:** In the pattern of shifting from region to region, the mobility is discursive. It may or may not be true to hypothesise that the labour would one day go back to their villages. There are exceptions and these are considerable. The case study presented below (of Maheshwar Das) explains the point.

3. Oscillation Across Sectors: If one were to identify three segments; agricultural sector, industrial sector, and other informal sector, or a relatively formal sector, relatively informal sector, based on concrete practices, a discursive mobility between these is what oscillation across sectors refers to the following case study provides the clue:

> N. Srinivas (31) was a worker in Professional Grades Components Ltd. A company producing electric circuits. They make carbon film resistors and metal film resistors. Sinivas was selected through an interview in 1985. He worked for one year as a trainee operator before being given the appointment letter. In 1991 India witnessed the opening of the economy. The flooding of cheap resistors from some of the south-east Asian countriesled to the closure of the industry. The workers were not paid any compensation. Now Srinivas has an electric shop where he repairs electric gadgets. One of his co-worker is driving a van in the town. Some of the migrants have joined other industries. Some other co-workers have joined back agriculture which they had left to join industry. In similar cases, Srinivas identifies workers who have set-up kirana shops.[2] It seems that shift from industrial employment offers a wide range of possibilities.

4. Oscillation Across Industry: An important dynamic of new-industrial labour market is that labour especially the growing majority of contractual and casual labour are shuttled between industries. There is no identification of labour with any particular industry. (This has an important consequence especially for organising labour.)[3]

> Srinivas (21) is a casual worker in Sangfroid industry. Srinivas belongs to the Reddy caste and is a short distance migrant from West-Godavari district. He has completed his intermediate with Biology, Physics and Chemistry as optional subjects. Now he is doing his Bachelor of Arts in distance education with Ambedkar Open University.[4] Srinivas's parents do not own any land but cultivate paddy on the land taken for share-cropping, after completing his intermediate, Srinivas came across an advertisement by Sangfroid Industries, seeking labour. Though no one else from his family

or his village have migrated as industrial labour, Srinivas however felt that since he is educated, he should not do agriculture. He worked for sometime in the local cotton mills. He therefore decided to venture into a new arena. He reached Adarshnagar the head-office of Sangfroid industry and appeared for the interview. In the interview, Srinivas was asked about his qualifications and experience. Srinivas had both. He was however asked to wait for a week for his result. Srinivas stayed during this period wit his friends who were studying in the city. After a week, Srinivas was given a letter inviting him to join the industry. As Srinivas had expected, he was offered rs. 1000/- per month for twelve hours of work with ESI and PF benefits and membership in 'Apadhbandhu[5], a credit society of the workers in this industry. Srinivas performs all the functions that contract labour perform, viz., capping, filling, sticking labels, checking, printing, etc. Sangfroid industries have three plants in Kothur viz., Sangfroid Phrma, Sangfroid Remedies, and JAS therapeutic. Workers, especially contract are usually freely interchanged with these units. The method of operation in case of the casual labour is different. Whenever these is lower manpower required in one plant, workers are asked to tender formal resignations in one plant and join the other. This leads to loss of a chance for being made permanent. Srinivas recounts that when JAS therapeutic a recent plant was started, the basic pay here was lower than what was being paid in Sangfroid Remedies. However, workers in Sangfroid Remedies were asked to resign and join JAS three years ago. Some of the casual workers declined to do so. The condition now is that the salaries of the workers who preferred to stay back have been stagnated as a punishment and those who joined JAS now draw more salaries.

The conditions of contract labour is much worse. Shuttling between industries is an everyday affair for them:

Ramlu (25) is a contract worker. He is a short distance migrant from Medak. He belongs to Madgiga caste. He has been trying to get employed in a pharmaceutical company every day. He stands outside the closed gates of the company from 4 a.m. and waits to be recruited. He is not alone, there is a huge crowed of workers before the company. It's a real war of war of voices-workers shouting as loudly as they can in desperation, to the contractor inside, to consider him or her for recruitment. The contactor has his own calculations. His contemplation do not have an exact pattern though they include considerations such as a minimum set of senior workers, workers known for efficiency, vulnerable workers (who are not particular about amount of wage) etc. or it could be considering a new one, or not disappointing someone who has been turned away a number of times already (for the contractor its 'god forbidden someone should not leave the market because they have lost faith, the hope is kept alive by making sure 'everybody gets a chance to survive' and only survive they will) it was an ill-facted day for Ramlu. He was turned away. It was almost 7 a.m. when he realised painfully he was not to get employed in that industry that day He was disappointed. But he is a witty man. He hangs up his arms and shouts loudly 'O my god, ippudu em cheyali nenu'[6] (O my god what should I do now) to the amusement of all his co-workers. It seemed, their laughter was an escape from crying. For those who do not find employment, it's a lost war. But in a moment he grows serious and curses the industry 'mudanna cheparu, ippudu vere chota kuda dorakadu' (these fellows don't inform us early enough to try in some other industry). If it were to be an hour before, he would have tried his luck on the door steps of another industry.

5. Oscillation Across Sections: Skill can be defined as an interaction between knowledge of the worker and the means of production. Skill is not a unified entity. It can be subdivided at-least into three qualitatively different stages. The first stage is interaction externally with tools. Second level is being part of a repetitive process. Knowing how to operate the machines. Third and the most crucial is possessing contingency knowledge. Knowing what to do when the machines don't do what they are supposed to do. Shuttling the workers from section to section with the factory in the name of multi-tasking and multi-skilling denies the labour an opportunity to pick-up contingency skills. The example below elucidates the point.

Shatrughan Singh (32) is working as a melter in Vinayaka Steels. He has 13 years of experience and draws a wage of Rs. 5000. His job includes supervision and technical work of setting temperatures of the furnace. Though, he has studied only upto 10th class, he has picked up the work from his seniors. In Shatrughan's case, being a sincere and hard workers, the senior electricians insisted that he be allowed to work continuously under them. First Shatrughan began by passing on the tools, later he began handling the machines. Now he knows a range of problems that the machines can face and how to rectify them. Shatrughan is however, amongst the few fortunate who got to learn a skill. Workers in the company are usually shuttled between different sections and remain as low paid unskilled helpers.

6. Oscillation Across Income: As is generally propounded by conventional economics, a worker will always prefer a better paid job than the one that he/she already has. However, in the context of the new-industrial labour, the workers are discoverers. They more from place to place in anticipation of a better wage but the market does not guarantee this, as workers do not always passes the right information. The varied kind of pressures also do not allow a linear upward mobility of wage in alternatives chosen. The case study (of Maheshwar Das) presented below clarifies the point.

7. Oscillation Across Social Milieu: Oscillation across social milieu is an obvious outcome of a regional oscillation when regions are multi-cultured. Multi-culturalism under certain conditions can add to beauty and richness of life. It is however important to take note of the point especially when multi-culturalism accentuates vulnerability. The following case studies (including the case of maheshwar Das) bring to fore this dimension effectively.

Maheswar Das (33) is a long distant migrant from Ghotua village in Baleswar district of Orissa. Maheshwar had no land and his father had grown old so in 1979 he had been to Calcutta to get recruited in the military the officials asked for Rs. 20,000 as bribe. He couldn't pay so he decided to work in some industry instead in 1980 went to a new township close to Bangalore to join as Bhatti[7] helper in Kusuma Alloys. He received Rs. 14000 for 8 hours of work. Once the Bhatti got punctured. The owner asked the Bhariman[8] for an explanation.

The Bhariman said "there are hospitals but not all save patients. Mistakes happen and accidents cannot be foreseen". The owner who took this explanation as a comment against him had a tussle with the worker and in what followed the Bhariman fell in the furnace and was burnt alive. Maheshwar says the owner intentionally pushed the worker in a fit of anger. The owner paid rupees hundred thousand as compensation to the bereaved family and got the case closed. Maheshwar Das went to Coembattore and joined in another steel plant as a timmerman[9] in 1982. He received a wage of Rs. 2200. After working for two years he received a telegram stating that his mother was serious. He stayed in the village for three months and when he came back he had lost his job. He had got Rs. 1000 from his village so he went to Dindigal in search of a job. Through a friend he approached a contractor in 1984 and got employed as a timmerman and received a wage of Rs. 3000 however after working for two years. Contractor ran away with last two months wage Maheshwar had to receive. Maheshwar felt cheated but could not do anything. With his savings he reached Madurai through another contractor in 1987 and got employed as a timmerman cum mould setter. He received a wage of Rs. 4000. Maheshwar Das decided to get married after working for two years and brought his family to Madurai. However soon he had to attended to his sister's delivery, it took him a month he lost his job. He reached Salem and worked as mason.

He got Rs. 1200 for 8 hours of work. He worked for six months and went to Houser in 1990 thinking that he would get a better deal but he had to work for 12 hours to get the same wage. He worked for three months. He then went to Palaghat through a friend and worked as a timmerman and received a wage of Rs. 3000. He worked for three years. On getting a better wage he went to Surath where he worked as a Timmerman and mould setter and received a wage a Rs. 5000 for 12 hours of work. However, in Surath most of the workers belonged to a community and he was the only Hindu. He was working well and his image was getting better when some workers belonging to other community approached him and threatened him. Maheshwar left the job and ironically went to Goa through a friend belonging to the other community. He worked as a Timmerman in 1997-98. However Maheshwar found that cost of living was high in Goa so he let the job and through a friend came to Vinayak steels in Kothur where he now receives Rs 3000. This case stands as an evidence of oscillation across regions, which is very obvious. The movement of wage from Rs. 4000 in Madurai to Rs. 1200 in salem and again an increase to Rs. 5000 in Surath and a decrease in Kothur to Rs. 3000 shows oscillation across income, mother's sickness and sister's delivery reflect the social pressures which produce such oscillation. The social relations in the township close to Bangalore and the context in Surath are obvicusly completely different this amounts to an oscillation across social milieu.

Mantu Kumar Singh (27) of Juranealpur village of Basali district in Bihar complains that because they do not know the local language, the shopkeepers and vegetable vendors cheat by quoting a higher price. He also says that he has suffered a cultural shock seeing women work along with men, whereas he does not allow his mother to go out of the house even to fetch water. Mantu has obviously been thrown into a new context without having a choice or a chance to prepare for it.

Devinidhi Eshwar (35) a Brahim from Begusria in Bihar working as a helper in a small scale industry which does printing on rexine cloth. The machinery for the industry was purchased in Faridabad. The then fitter of the machines who came to Kothur to fix the machine brought Eshwar with him. Now Eshwar has fifteen years of experience and draws a salary of Rs. 2898. He migrated along with his wife. Eshwar's wife is a reserved person. Having parted with family and friends and relatives and not being allowed to move freely in the township, within a few years of stay, unable to bear the tree of the new atmosphere. Ehwar' wife developed pychological problem. He ha bout of depression when she starts uncontrollably crying. Eshwar has to take her to a psychiatrist during such periods. Obviously Ehwar' wife ha a low threshold limit to take in the oscillation across social milieu under oppressive conditions.

8. Oscillation Across Resource: Oscillation across resource is an important dimension. It reflects the operation of the multiple-identity conflicts in the social context. A resource can be defined as an entitlement which can lead to an upward mobility of labour, in a vertical socio-economic scale. However, a resource cannot be strictly defined as a resource for all moments. What is a resource at a moment for labour may well turn-out to be a liability, a constraint at another. The case study below clarifies the point.

> Nirakar Vishwal (24) is a contract labourer in Vinayaka Steels Industry conditions at home forced Vishwal to migrate. He was also aware that agriculture was not very remunerative and searching for opportunities outside can fetch higher income. Villages of Bhadrak, Cuttak and Gangam Districts know F.M. Nayak's family very well. He is a well known labour contractor of that area. Nirakar went with his friend belonging to the same village who knew the contractor. Nirakar inquired with him if he could give him some work, the contractor agreed. Nirakar joined the steel plant as a helper, (where most of the workers are from Bihar, U.P., M.P. and Orissa) in 1994 and was paid Rs. 1100 per month. When Nirakar first joined work he was petrified with the conditions. Working in conditions of extreme heat throughout the day and lifting heavy weights made him not only feel weak but also suffer from body pains. However, Nirakar thought to himself that he would not return to his village as a failure and that increased his will power to stay back at Kothur and continued to work. It took him three months to settle down. After working for six months his wage increased to Rs. 1200. After 8-10 months Nirakar learnt work fast and became a maistry (mason) in the steel industry. He drew a wage of Rs. 1600. During the summer there are frequent power cuts for long intervals workers are free during this period. Some workers got an idea that during this time they could play. Workers put some money collectively and bought a bat ball and wickets. The minimum resources necessary to start a game of cricket. The team consisted of all Oriya people. It was also during this period that the Oriya community staying in Kothur was celebrating Ganesh puja. So the participants decided to name their team as Ganapathy cricket club. While they were playing they were approached by the locals to play tournaments. This got Nirakar in touch with the locals. He became close to a Telugu boy named Shanker who was working in a Batteries company HBL as a casual worker. From him Nirakar came to know that technical work rather than manual work is more far fetching in terms of career opportunities. Through Shankar, Nirakar joined the HBL company as a fitter which as a technical post. The company predominantly had teleugus[10]

as they are better known amongst the migrants. Nirakar found to his dismay that the locals were teaching only their community people technical work. Nobody was taking interest in Nirakar. Nirakar felt left-out. He joined back the steel plant again after two months. The regional identity which was initially a resource, in the sense that it played an important role in Nirakar finding a job in the steel company, became a constraint when it came to another type of work in another industry. There is in this sense an oscillation across resource.

Oscillating labour, as a concept, is an acknowledgement of the increasing unpredictability of the labour markets. Oscillating labour are the unprotected workers devoid of even minimum rights in the labour market. This however is not new in the economy as a whole. What all new industries have done is they have opened up the protected formal sector workers to the uncertain rural labour markets. In a way it has opened up the question of rural poverty and deprivation in the manufacturing industrial sector. It has brought into question the silence of industrial trade unions about the misery of the rural poor for all these years However, for the workers themselves this has meant deep social crisis. Some of the cases reflecting this crisis are given below:

SECTION—IV

The Growing Social Crisis

The social ties have been the shock absorbing mechanism for the poor in the times of crisis. Family, relatives and friends have often been the mechanisms to fight vulnerability. One would expect a similar situation in the new-industrial towns. However, it is increasingly becoming clear that the pressures of various kinds that are exerted in the newlabour markets are pushing social ties into crisis. Firstly, one needs to take note of the fact that there is a shift in the perception of relations in the countryside within the family as a result of migration. For families young men and women are no longer mere sons and daughters but a source of living—an asset. This is coming to be the predominant identity. To be happy with what one has is no longer the philosophy of life. To grow, to accumulate is the objective. This has a serious implication that relations are becoming increasingly instrumentalist owing to socio-economic pressures. Apart from this, contacts with unknown people and entering into a family relations without complete information have often led to bad outcomes especially for women. Women however are seen taking the risk because some families are unable to perform the role of networking for marriages because of extreme poverty and exclusion. Further, as social ties become increasingly instrumentalist, there is an increase in the number of cases of opportunistic behaviour. Following case studies are intended to present the alarming path which the institutions based on social ties have taken.

> Suresh (14) is a contract worker in Sangfroid industry. He belongs to Gouda caste and is a short distance migrant from Shamshabad Mandal of R.R. District. Suresh has studied up to 7th class. Suresh's contractor has manipulated his age as 19 years ad taken him into work. Suresh's father passed away when Suresh was very young. It is his mother, his sister and his two brothers who brought him up by working as agricultural labourers. Suresh's mother owns half acre of land. Suresh's sister has studied up to 10th class however she did not find any better employment than Suresh. In the backdrop of conditions at home, Suresh's mother felt that there is no purpose education serves and therefore discontinued Suresh's education and made him join as a contract worker in the hope that he would earn and expenditure on his education can be avoided. Suresh who loves to play cricket, see moves, chat with friends has to now wake up at 4 a.m. and work till 6 p.m. Suresh has lost his childhood.

> C. Lakshmi (30) is a casual worker in a ceramics industry. Fourteen years ago she came across a co-worker—Venkataiah and they got married. When Lakshmi got married, she did not have much information about Venkataiah since he was from Andhra region. The reason she married him was because she

thought he was a very enterprising and a good person. A year later, Lakshmi gave birth to a boy. They named him Yadgiri. When Yadgiri was one year old, his father eloped with another village to Andhra region deserting him and his mother. Lakshmi says that this is not a stray incident. Many marriages between unknown people are breaking down.

Shantamma (35) belongs to the Madiga caste and hails from Nandigama village in Kothur Mandal. She was only thirteen when she was married. After one year, Shantamma's husband passed away. However, by that time Shantamma had gone birth to a female child. After her husband's death, Shantamma was dependant on her brothers and mother. Her brother and mother got Shantamma married again to a man who was already married but could not have children from his first wife. Shantamma, adjusted well with the first wife of her second husband. Soon Shantamma had two daughters from her second husband. However, the context changed when Shantamma's second husband's first wife gave birth to a boy. Shantamma's husband started ill-treating her. He used to abuse and beat her and her daughters without any apparent reason. So, Shantamma decided to take her daughters and migrate to her home town—Nandigama and started her life as a casual labourer in a ceramics industry.

Menana (35) is a female casual worker in a ceramics industry. She hails from Kothur and belongs to the Lambada tribe. She and her husband were working in Bombay. They used to send money order in the name of her husband's brother who had the duty of depositing the money in their name. Menaka has three children. Menaka realised that in Bombay cost of education was very high and she could not get her children educated. She therefore decided to comeback to Kothur along with her children. After coming she approached her husband's brother for her savings. It came as a rule shock when Menaka realised that her husband's brother was a cheat. She says their hard earned labour was lost because a very close relative had turned selfish.

M. Krishna (40) is a permanent worker of a Ceramics industry. He is from Appareddugudam village in Kothur and belongs to Medari (basket weaving) caste. Krishna's greatest worry is that he has to get his four daughters marked. He recently got his first daughter married, for which he spent Rs. 20,000/-. In order to be able to give dowry and perform the marriages,

Krishna does multiple jobs. Apart from his permanent job from which he earns Rs. 2085/- per month, he owns sixteen acres of land which he has given for share-cropping. He along with his family also engages in his caste occupation of basket weaving. He has to work in the factory, supervise the land and sell baskets. All these workers keep him engaged throughout the day and all through the week. He says that life has become so hectic that he and his family are unable to attend any social gatherings in the relatives circle. This has led to misunderstandings between his relatives and his family.

Shiva Kumar (21) is a casual worker in a cement pipes industry. He is a local and belongs to Telaga caste (B.C.) Abject poverty Shiva kumar to discontinue his education when he was in his 2nd class and join the labour market as an agricultural labourers. Because of his father's addiction to sarai (country liquor) the family had to sell-off the two acres of land to clear debts. Added to this, Shiva Kumar's sister who was married-off was sent back because Shiva Kumar's family had failed to pay the complete dowry amount which was Rs. 10,000/- and ten tulas (ten grams) of gold.

Damodar Jhatai (56) is a long distance migrant from Patsalo village of Bhadrak district in Orissa. He approached a contractor who happened to be in the same village and came to work in a steel industry in Kothur. Damodar decided not to get his family because if family joins him, he has to rent a room. Damodar now stays in a asbestos roofed 10 feet by 10 feet room (along with two others) provided by the company. It is now ten years since Damodar has migrated. He has grown old and feeble. Once Damodar decided to quit work and relax. However, conditions at home do not allow him to rest. Family is unable to take care of him.

Sughunath Malik (28) is a long distant migrant worker from bhamkura village in Bhadrak district of Orissa who is working in a steel industry. Through one of his friends who had contacts, Sughunath approached a contractor and managed to find work in Kothur in 1989. Sugunath is employed in the loading section. In this section, workers have to load ingots which are five feet long five inches this iron rods weighing about 70-75 kgs into trucks which are then transported to the rolling mills for which ingots are the raw materials. Sugunath's job also involves dressing the ingots, dressing involves breaking the unwanted fittings to the ingots with a hammer. Sughunath's job involves hard labour and he works for twelve hours a day beginning from 8 a.m. to 8 p.m. In 1991 Sughunath got married. However, he did not get his family to Kothur for the next three years. However, he had three children in these years. Having living without a family, Sughunath like most of his friends started drinking and visiting prostitutes. In 1995 Sughunath got his wife and children to Kothur. However, he kept visiting the prostitutes. One such visit ended up in a misadventure. Sughunath, along with two of his friends who were locals went to a prostitute. They settled for a bargain. However, both of his friends who were in a drunken state disregarded the bargain and forcefully had a sexual intercourse with the lady. The lady registered a case of rape. Since both his friends were locals, they somehow managed to escape. In the process Sughunath got implicated in the case and was sent to jail, where he spent the next seven months. During all these years Sughunath's wife was alone with Sughnath's brother. Even before Sughnath came out of the prison he faced another rude shock—his wife eloped with his brother. Sugunath's friends feel that since, Sughunath was unable to give enough attention to his family, it collapsed.

Crime as a Consequence of Crisis

In a number of companies, the managements have stopped co-operating with the unions. The labour recently has seen ill-treatment, discrimination, in the companies. The unions have failed to draw-up new wage agreements. There was an underlying anger amongst the workforce against the owners, managers and also some of the supervisors of different factories. On the day of a recent Bandh call given by the INTUC as a mark of respect for the death of a Congress leader, the Congress activists, predominantly workers went on a targeted rampage. They attacked the companies which were not co-operating and beat-up the most hated managers and supervisors through-out the industrial town. This instance was both a mechanism of spreading terror by the Mafia, it certainly was a recent instance of ventilation of anger and frustration by the workers. This incident does suggest failure of the democratic institutions.

The growing general crime rate in the Kothur town over the years is also suggestive of a growing frustration of the local poor who no longer seem to be finding opportunities in the new industries. The total number of crimes murder, robbery, kidnaps etc. recorded in the Kothur police station sees a general rise with 97 cases reported in the year 1996, 155 cases in the year 1997, 104 cases in the year 1998, 121 cases in the year 1999, 143 cases in the year 2000. The crime has to be understood in the backdrop of the growing crisis. This does cause concern. In fact the crisis has reached a point where the institutions meant to prevent crime are resorting to crime themselves. The recent episode of police violence in the town causes concern:

The local Sub-inspector (SI) of Police accompanied a private construction contractor to a new steel industry and demanded 14 tonnes of steel free of cost for the construction of the local police station. The owner's son who was present at the spot declined to give it, stating that in a earlier occasion 3 tonnes were given at a reduced price to a friend of the SI and said that since the company is new, it cannot afford to give such huge quantities free of cost. There was an argument and the SI slapped the owner's son. The contractor who was also part of the ruling party left the place and went to the Kothur town and got with him few youngsters who then attacked the owner's son. Sensing the danger, the owner's son escaped in his car. The police and the contractor's men chased the owner's son and caught hold of him in an adjacent village. He was then taken to Shadnagar police station. The same evening it is said that the police bought the local media persons of leading regional language news papers by distributing money and got the news carried as if the owner's son attempted to murder the SI and the villagers protected him. The same evening the owner's son was paraded half naked in the town and was continuously beaten. The owner's son collapsed at a point of time and become unconscious. He was made to stand and was offered cool drinks and was beaten again. The same evening the Superintendent of Police visited the town and honoured those youth who supported the police. The owner turned out to be a relative of the proprietor of a leading regional daily news paper. On the behest of the owner, the news paper sent a journalist from the main office and got the case investigated. The next day the real reasons for the assault were reported. The news paper suspended the local news reporter. Mass rallies were held in the city asking the government to take action against the police. After few weeks of massive campaign, the police officials directly responsible for the assault were suspended from their jobs. On enquiry from reliable sources it was said that the SI who was new to the area was under instruction from the Deputy Superintendent of Police in Shadnagar to collect a certain amount of money regularly as extortion and to contribute it to him. Since the Si was new to the area he was harassing everyone and it was as part of this larger process of pilferage that the SI grew increasingly indiscriminate. It also needs to be noted that the acts of the SI were condoned by the SP. These were the main reasons for the above episode. No action was taken against the DSP, however, public pressure was so much that the SP was transferred.

The above episode is suggestive of the enormous arbitrary authority that institutions such as the police have come to enjoy. Part of the reason lies in the ambiguity of rules due to growing informality wherein the industrialists are allowed to break laws and in exchange the Labour. Excise, Pollution Control Board and Police officials are getting kickbacks from the profit so incurred. Apart from this institutional crisis, there is also a crisis in the civil society. What follows tries to focus on this aspect.

These great social-psychological costs that workers pay may be termed as Vulnerability costs often not considered by the mainstream economists. In the context of systematic disorganisation of labour, a process of annihilation of trade unions, are there any alternative institutions to protect worker's right? The next section tries to focus on this aspect.

Other forms of Social Crisis: The fourth chapter presented case studies suggestive of the deep social crisis that the society is passing through in terms of breakdown of social ties. Other forms of crisis are manifest by instances such as the selling of female infants by Lambada tribes because of extreme poverty. It needs to be noted that Lambadas are considerable in number amongst the workers and are employed in some of the worst forms of employment. For example all the workers employed as daily contract workers in Vinayak steels are Lambadas. The gender dimension as part of this social crisis comes up very clearly, especially in the fact that women are victims of breakdown of families. However, there are instance where men have also suffered. The following case study manifests another kind of crisis.

> Begum is a Muslim, aged 20. She is an illiterate and is working as a casual labourer in garden section of NCL from past one year. She draws a salary of Rs. 40/- per day. Begum lost her mother in her childhood and her father married another lady. Begum's step mother got her married to a blind man who is considerably old when compared to Begum. Begum is a pretty young lady. After her marriage she started living with her husband in his own house in Nandigaon. She had 3 kids soon after her marriage, who are now in school. Begum faced harassment (Both physical and mental) from her husband, right from the beginning of her marriage. He used to suspect her of misconduct. Though they had considerably healthy economy in form of rents from their house, because of the growing necessities Begum had to take up the work in NCL factory. Added to her pathetic situation at house, she had to face a grave situation at the factory. Due to some financial problems she applied for a loan of rs. 500/- in the factory. As a matter of convention the section supervisor approves the requisition for loan before it reaches the higher officials, hence, Begum's requisition was in the supervisor's hands. Her

supervisor Mr. Yadaiah, asked her to meet him in the store room. Begum was new to the factory. Further, except her, there are no female workers in the gardening section. It is therefore that during the working hours, she has no access to her friends. She had to approach the supervisor alone. Taking this as an opportunity, Yadaiah closed the doors of the room, assaulted her, threatened her and raped her. She says he warned her not to reveal this to any body as she might lose her job as well as her dignity in society. However Begum couldn't keep the tragedy happened to her and shared it with one of her fellow female workers who knew her personal life and her problems. Yadaiah is a leader of INTUC, INTUC leaders feel that the opposition union BMS is trying to gain political mileage out of the issue. Some of the activist groups such as the 'tree Chaitanya Sravanthi' took this issue highlighting it as a struggle for female worker's right to 'Dignity' and want Begum to come forward and launch a complaint with the factory management to see to it that Yadaiah is punished. Initially, Begum was interested in reporting this injustice done to her to the management. But, because of the pressure and harassment back at home, and the fear of social consequences she is not in a position to come forward openly. She also says that, she was beaten up black and blue by her husband who because suspicious because of the rumours. Begum sustained serious injuries on her face. Her face had swelling all over her right side and she had to bunk her duty which ultimately ended up in added financial instability. Now Begum's husband stopped eating food cooked by her. He cooks on his own and now he treats her as an untouchable in the house. Even her children are kept away from her after this incident.

Such instances of injustice are also a result of the insecurity suffered by workers owing to the informal employment. It is also a result of failure of institutions such as the trade unions.

SECTION—V

Challenging the Market's Madness

It is maintained that "the misery that is attributed to the failure of what is pejoratively called 'development

Economics', meaning state interventionism, it took decades for that distress to unfold. But the structural adjustment programme (SAP), under the Counter Revolution, has unleashed within a very short span, a market-driven growth which is 'jobless, ruthless, voiceless, rootless and futureless" (UNDP, 1996 as in D. Narasimha Reddy, 2002). It is further stated that "while these indications are the distinction of salvaging theory, it should be emphasised that 'development', after all, is an area that has no meaning if it is not translated into action, which is invariable political action, "really important factors in 'development' are 'political'. Because, political change seemed difficult, if not impossible, to achieve through reform, the obvious answer seemed to be the need to start change through political revolution." (D. Narasimha Reddy, 2002). Added to this there is no human side and cultural side to the market which can protect institutions and practices of solidarity which in essence are the true sources of protecting labour rights. The sources of challenge to the madness of the market come from different pockets. Movements, Struggles, and Resistances such as the radical left movements in the rural pockets of Andhra, Bihar and Orissa from where the migrants are coming from have had an impact on the wages and quality of employment of the agricultural labour (Arvind Das). These movements have also had significant impact on the wages and production relations in the most backward regions of Telangana. Caste movements have also taken up issues relating to poverty apart from fighting their main battle for dignity. The gender movements have also had a role in challenging oppressive patriarchal structures and thereby have contributed significantly to the changing production and cultural relations. The environmental movements have had an important role in checking the irresponsible industrialisation and have in a way contributed to challenging the model of development. In Kothur move specifically, the Stree Chaitanya Samakhya, Andhra Pradesh Civil Liberties Committee, Dalit Seva Samiti, Telangana Jana

Sabha, Christian Missionaries, and other NGOs to name a few are organisations which have contributed to the betterment of human relations. The separate Telangana movement especially has raised important regional issues and has directly addressed some of the fundamental problems relating to the regional disparities. However, these movements as of now have a limited reach. The informal resistance by the workers both collectively and individually as is presented in the fourth chapter are some other identifiable sources of hope for the workers to improve their conditions. There is a need for creative social movements fighting the market madness to not only fight the blind faith in privatisation and competition but also actively co-opt the welfare state. Such a strategy in this context would perhaps mean at least performing those function of social protection that informal market institutions are performing. At times they have to act as facilitators, at times as lobbies and at times as movements. However, given the oppressive working environments, and certain traditional cultural practices, which reduce social space for creative action how these struggles can converge creatively learning from their experience and transform the reality taking on the challenges posed by it, inclusive of the wellbeing of different conflicting sections of the society and what expression such a convergence would find in redefining the purpose and content of development will be interesting to observe.

REFERENCES

1. Grocery shop
2. Grocery shop
3. There can no longer be in the long run factory based unions, because of contractualisation and casualisation, there is no stable relation between industrial units and labour. The unions have to be located in the social realm and cut across specific factories.

4. What can be a better tribute to the contributions of Prof.. G. Ram Reddy.

5. 'Apadha' in telugu means danger or crisis. 'Bandhu' means a friend. 'Apadhbandhu' means a friend in moments of danger or crisis.

6. Imitating Nageshwar Rao, a Telugu film star.

7. Furnance

8. Bhariman is the worker who forks the iron-ore into the furnace. This is a semi-skilled job and involves working in extreme heat and exposed to hazards.

9. Timmerman is the worker who removes slag which comes to the surface when iron-ore melts in the furnance. It is a semi-skilled job and involves working in extreme heat and exposed to hazards.

10. The Telugu speaking people belonging to the state of Andhra Pradesh.

11. I would like to thank my supervisors Prof. Jan Breman, Prof. Henk Thomas, and Prof. D. Narasimha Reddy and a lifetime supervisor Prof. G. Haragopal who have been a great source of inspiration. Their humane personalities have a compelling reflection in my research. I would also like to thank Prof. R. Radhakrishna, Prof. I.S.A. Baud, Dr. Schiphorst, Dr. peter Knorringa, Mr. S.R. Sankaran, Dr. K. Balagopal, K.G. Kanabiran, Dr. Arun, Patnaik, G. Ajay, and Sumi whose comments have enriched the paper. Thanks are due to Ank. V.D. Berg, Dr. Balasubrahmaniam, Mr. Harshawardhan, Mr. Venugopal Goud, Mr. Sujan Vathsal, Mr. Venkateshwar Rao who have been a great source of support. Thanks are particularly due to my mother, Dr. M. Vanamala, for all that she has done to deal with difficult circumstances during my research.

11

Human Rights and Structural Adjustment Programme with Special Reference to Rights of Workers

Mrs. N. Rajeswari

Introduction

Humans are not only social animals, but also beigns with a will to lead a life of hard work and labour, with a desire to live out of one's toils. Production of goods, and a livelihood out of such efforts has been the tale of man from time immemorial. Even before the so-called "society" formed, man had the responsibility to make a living with his partner, and take care of his off springs. The one element that he acquries right from birth, is his human right. While many eminent Human Rights activists have been quoted often, a person acquries human rights the day he is born, his fight to retain it also starts almost simultaneously. After thousands of years of existence, we are yet to ring in a state where human rights are protected and restored. Infringements on human rights have been carried on ceaselessly, in the name of religion, industrialisation, progress, globalisation, and now SAP. To quote the UN General Secretary Kofi Annan—"Billions of people are still trying to survive on less than Rs 130/- a day. With no drinking water, health care of access to education, still denied the jobs that would help them escape their improverished state, and thus, still deprived of some of the most basic rights...". It is ironic that the third world countries in their bid to struggle out of viscous circles emulate policies that may have worked elsewhere. Worst still they incorporate plans that have dubious records and are known to have failed elsewhere, in a desperate hope that everything will somehow work out better, and "click" for an assured future.

Third world countries have been implementing short-term macro economic stablisation and long-term structural adjustment programmes. These measures often lead to disasters such as redundancy, under employment and unemployment and an overall degeneration of the economy. If we consider the majority of the populace of a country to be involved in labour, direct or indirect, then we have to realise that these people not only produce but also consume. The workers should not be eyed as mere producers, but in sheer numbers they also are important consumers. Policies that hurt them will hurt the nation. If a State cannot provide for its work force, it cannot boast of development. If the majority of the population is below the poverty line, then policies must certainly be focused to give a thrust to this sector to elevate them above the line, and not merely twiddle with the line in rhetoric. The current scenario in our country is alarming enough as it is, and to top this all, if there is a political will to support SAP, we are headed towards a dead end. One may count this as one more of the miseries heaped by policy-makers on the common man, but for the implications of these policies directly on human rights, and all the good it represents.

There is an attempt made in this paper to look at the serious problems posed by SAP, especially in reference to the rights of workers. After all is it not the sage truth that despite heavy mechanisation and modernisation, men are always required to run these machines? Then, is it not the duty of the state to safeguard the interests of such a force?

Structural Adjustment Programme

Like many jargons before, SAP gives one a nice feeling when one rolls their tongue over it. But as a new concept it is not without conscious vagueness. Often used in the context of "Global Transformation" it would signify to the third world country trade and investment liberalisation in the immediate period and domination as a part of long term adjustments. One can understand here that structural adjustment is meant as an adjustment of the economics of the less developed countries to suit the changes taking place in the highly developed capitalist countries. Structural Adjustment, therefore, may be seen as having three important dimensions viz.

(a) Adjustment from existing system of protected trade towards free trade and investment.

(b) Shift from an economic order dominated by public sector towards primacy of private sector, and

(c) Shift of emphasis from capital goods production to consumption goods production.

Structural adjustment, thus, seems to be banking heavily on the premise that privatisation and free trade together would bring about improved efficiency, competitiveness and faster growth. It does this by referring to the inefficiencies of public sector and its lack of adaptability to the changing world economic scenario, the inappropriateness of protected trade and the unsuitability of factors like land, labour, capital and enterprise in developing countries. What if history reveals that India did have a period before independence where private sector was dominating, and free trade and the industrial sector was confined to consumer goods. Even more revealing is lack of such elements as competitiveness, efficiency and faster growth.

The typical components of an orthodox structural adjustment programme are macroeconomic policies of fiscal stringency, monetary contraction and devaluation at one level. On the second level is sectoral and micro economic policies which is characterised by the deregulation of labour markets, financial markets and agricultural prices and removal of trade barriers. The goal seems to be to minimize Governmental involvement under the guise that the State is not such an efficient producer. What if studies elsewhere has alarmingly revealed that SAP leaves the poor poorer in the short run.

Human Rights

"All Human Rights for All" is a slogan coined in the recent years, and proclaimed vociferously on all platforms. That a person has human rights from the day he is born is stating the obvious. History of mankind is replete with horrendous tales of human right's infringements, and laws have been made and modified so many times that some of the words and concepts have totally lost meaning and context. Yet rationale demands that law is the only recourse to redress. There is an ever increasing realisation that laws are necessary to remove barriers to freedom of participation, expression, and association, but to implement them effectively will require not only resources, but a political will. Not only should the marginalised be empowered to protect their rights, but there must be created an enabling environment for such a change to take place.

Productive and satisfying livelihoods give people the means to buy goods and services. They empower people socially by enhancing their dignity and self-esteem and they can empower people politically by enabling them to influence decision-making in the work place and beyond. In industrial countries most workers are employed in the formal labour market in developing countries most are outside the formal labour market.

The Universal Declaration of Human Rights recognises the right to work, to freely choose employment and to have just and favourable working conditions. All these rights are reiterated in the International covenant on Economic. Social and Cultural Rights, which also emphasises the obligation of parties to the covenant to safeguard rights to work so that everyone has the opportunity to ern a living.

Our constitution provides adequate rights to our workers through rights to work, without discrimination, with equal pay for equal work, and just and favourable remuneration ensuring human dignity and social protection.

SAP vs Rights of Workers

Structural Adjustment Programme may have good effects ostensibly on all areas of economy, as believed and projected by policy makers, but surely it has an adverse effect on the human rights issues related to workers. If carefully examined, the results of introducing SAP could be

- Increase in price of food grains due to reduction of subsidy on agricultural inputs.
- Devaluation of currency giving a further boost to the spiralling prices.
- External trade liberalisation may lead to more exports resulting in a play of supply and demand mismatch and thus increase in prices.
- Raising fuel and transformation costs will lead to welfare losses for the poor.

All these changes in the prices of essential commodities would directly affect the poorer sections and deprive them of adequate consumption of these commodities.

With the emphasis clearly on encouraging privatisation and the private sector which runs more on the "hire and fire" policies, this shift in focus is bound to result in retrenchments, layoffs, exist policies, golden handshakes; by whatever name mentioned, an attempt to get rid of manpower. The loss of jobs, and non-availability of new employment opportunities together are likely to cause serious distress in worker's interest. Low and falling income levels are a chronic problem for poor people in poor societies. These chronic conditions are often accentuated following recession and adjustment as unemployment increases as does the prices of food. This directly affects the human rights of the workers.

A separate board constituted under the name of "Board for Industrial and Financial Reconstruction" attempts to review those units declared sick, and assist in closing terminally sick units, at the same time checks indiscriminate closure of units. But essentially workers are bound to lose their jobs while the management takes cover under one loopholes or the other and ensure closure of units.

A National Renewal Fund set up by the Government attempts to create a fund for Employment Generation and Insurance fund for employees. This attempt is not only to pay those employees who have been given a golden handshake, but also provide soft loans for them to set up alternative sources of income. Very little is done towards ensuring job security and consistency.

Apart from loss of employment, SAP will also result in deprivation of facilities which is mandatory and a definite responsibility of the State to provide to every individual of the society viz., right to education, health, drinking water, sanitation and other social services. The experience of introducing SAP in South Africa and Latin America has revealed that it brings in its wake extensive deprivation to the poorer segments of the society. The Human Development Reports have been referring to SAP as one which emphasise market driven growth which leads in "unless worthless voiceless, rootless and future less growth".

Even the short period of experience in India suggests that the raising prices, the increasing process on subsidies to public distribution system, the limited allocation of funds to education and health care have all actually worsened the situation of poverty in India.

UNICEF has strongly advocated the implementation of SAP with a human face. It basically means depriving the rights, but at the same time attempting to soften the blow. Does it really improve the situation any? Safety nets such as supplying food at a subsidized price through the public distribution system (which is already in existence), providing "Mass public employment programmes" to ward off the effects of "Exit Policies" and to reallocate funds to those services that reach the poor directly. Safety nets in the field of education can only guarantee education at "elementary and secondary level". The implementation of these safety nets have been fraight with severe constraints of resources, inability to properly target the beneficiary groups, half-hearted attempts at employment generation, providing facilities for health, education and other services. The consequences are, thus, not only limited to workers and their rights, but the right to life itself. All these feeble "motions" only undermine the efforts of the UN in human development, while it opens the floodgates to the World Bank and the IMF to forcibly take over the reins of the country. Poor countries are unlikely to take on a large country on fear of consequences in areas beyond trade, such as aid, debt relief and export credits.

Conclusion

In conclusion while SAP may not be the solution to the problems faced by India through the globalisation, there can be solutions, if we take time and effort to perceive and pursue:

- The Industries in India must have a social responsibility instead of profits as their only driving force.

- People who are policy makers and involved in the governance of the country must acquaint themselves of the facts and realities at the grass-root levels.
- Problems that the country faces should not be merely communicated to the public, but the governing machinery must put efforts to sensitise people to these issues, so that they can be viewed in the correct perspective.
- The strategies adapted by the State must essentially relate to and be in context with the situation in our country, both cultural and environmental and must not be hashed up and poor imitation of a success story elsewhere.

At the micro level, the problem can be tackled by:

- Making a course on Economics and Economic Policies compulsory to everybody at a higher secondary level, and above.
- Employers must be oriented towards the problems and the rights of the workers, and at the same time be made aware of the economic policies in simple and easy to understand modes.
- Policymakers and Law makers should introduce transparency in whatever they do, so that they can collect responses from the cross section of the society before coming to a conclusion.
- Law to be implemented on a Rights based approach which will instill confidence in and respect for law amidst the common man.

At the macro level the problems needs to be looked at:

- Approach to governance to give due attention to the minorities, especially the labour force in an informal sector.

- State to act via media between the international organisations and the internal society and individuals of a country.
- To focus on all issues that affect worker's rights and problems to be discussed with people who have actually worked at grass root levels and are thus aware of the ground realities.

Ultimately what is required to improve worker's rights in developing countries are investments and economic growth that create jobs, stronger national laws and their implementation, and adaptation of higher standards by the domestic private sector and the foreign investors. Sanctions, and even threats of a penalty may change Government policies around. But basically, worker's rights depend upon the behaviour of individual employers, which again depends on how effectively laws are implemented. It is time we converted rhetoric to reality.

REFERENCES

1. Dr. Subramanian S. *Human Rights—International Challenges,* Manas Publications, New Delhi-110002, 1997.
2. Ginneken Van Wouter. *Social Security for all Indians,* Oxford University Press, Delhi, 1998.
3. UNDP Human Development Report, Oxford university Press, 2000.
4. The Indian Journal of Labour Economics. Conference Issue, Indian Society of Labour Economics, New Delhi, Vol 44, No. 4, Oct-Dec 2001.

12

Human Right Viewpoint of Environment

Prof. V. Hemalatha Devi
& B. Yuvakumar Reddy

Introduction

Man is both a nature and moulder of his environment, which gives him physical sustenance and affords him the opportunity for intellectual, moral, social and spiritual growth. In the long and torturous evolution of human race on this planet, a stage has been reached when through the rapid acceleration of science and technology; man has acquired the power to transform his environment in countless ways and an unprecedented scale. Both aspects of man's environment the natural and man make one essential to his well-being and the enjoyment of basic human rights, even the right to life itself.

International Scene

Universal Declaration of Human Right-1948 is the foundation upon which the modern conception of Human Rights has been built. An activist state is one which takes interest in all forms of the activities of their subjects sometimes may be leading to undue interference. Human rights are of crucial significance and are basic to human welfare and prosperity.

Human rights are inseparable from human life and human beigns since human existence without right is of no meaningful. Every individual must enjoy freedoms, which are fundamental to this growth and purposive life.

The term 'Environment' may be defined as 'environment' includes water, air and land and the interrelationship which exists among and between water, air and land and human beings, other living creatures, plants, micro-organism and property'.

Though there is inter-relationship and intergenerational interdependence between the environment and human existence, at present it is very much essential to visualise the concept of environment with a human right viewpoint of perspective.

Universal Declaration of Human rights, 1948, which consists of 30 Articles, does not provide direct provision on Environment. But certain provisions indirectly deal with it viz everyone has the right to life, liberty and security of person and every one has the right to a standard of living adequate for the health and well-being of himself and his family, including food, clothing, housing and medical care and necessary social services and the right to security in the event of unemployment sickness, disability, widowhood, old age or other lack of livelihood in circumstances beyond his control.[2] The first United Nations conference on Human Environment was held in Stockholm in 1972 to draft the Magna Carta of Environmentalism, popularly known as Stockholm Declaration. In that conference the phase human environment was well discussed and the declaration emphasised on the protection and improvement of human environment.

On the basis of Stockholm Declaration Indian constitution was amended[3] to include specific provision on environment namely Article 48-A one of the Directive Principles of State Policy and Article 51-A(g) one of the fundamental duties of citizens. It is very clear that environmentalism has been clearly linked with human rights. Right to live is one of the fundamental rights[4], which has been acclaimed even in Stockholm.

In 1983, the Brundtland Commission, the World Commission on Environment and Development was formed to investigate means to meet the needs of the rapidly growing population in a sustainable manner.

The historic Earth Summit held in Rio-De Jeneiro (Brazil) in 1992, adopted the Rio Declaration on Environment and Development. The Declaration stated that human beings were at the centre of concern for sustainable development and set the goal of establishing a new and equitable global partnership through the creation of new levels of co-operation among states, key sectors of society, and people. Right to development should be fulfilled so as to equitably meet the developmental and environmental needs of the present and future generations.

The facilitation of public awareness of environmental issues by the state was emphasised which indirectly meant public right too have information access to judicial and administrative proceedings including redress and remedy, should also be provided. This shows that right to healthy life of all species, present and future and right to development in sustainable manner were well recognised in the Rio-summit.

Agenda 21 provides for the protection and promotion of human health, promotioning provisions of Environmental infrastructure, water, sanitation, drainages and solid waste management which ultimately reflects the right to public health and holesome environment. Emphasis was laid on rights. Right to compensation was recognised through Polluter pays Principle'.

Involving women actively in Environment decision making at all levels, integrate gender concerns and perspectives in policies and programmes for sustainable development were considered in the Beijing Women's Conference 1995.

Indian Scene

The Indian Constitution is amongst the few in the world that contains specific provisions on Environmental protection. The Directive Principles of State Policy[5] and Fundamental Duties[6] enunciate national commitment to protect and improve environment. It is true that environment has not been included under Part III of the constitution, which deals with fundamental rights. But its reflections in Directive Principles and Fundamental duties show the mind of the Constitution hence it can be recognised as a human right by all means.

Article 21[7] of the Constitution ensures the persons protection of law. It is well established that 'law is not whatever the legislature enacts. Maneka Gandhi's[8] case formulates that law means a reasonable law.

Environmental policy making like other controversial areas of public policy is a never-ending process and the courts will always be intimately involved in this process. The increase in environmental awareness since 1980s has triggered a spirit in the environmental cases reaching the courts. 'It is emphatically the province and duty of the judiciary to say what the law is.[9]

The environmental petitions are generally based on the plea of violation of fundamental rights. It was not until 1978 that the Supreme Court breathed substantive life in to Article 21 by subjecting state action interfering with life or liberty to a test of reasonableness requiring not only that the procedures be authorised by law but that they are 'right, just and fair'. This transformation paved the way for a substantive reinterpretation of constitutional and legal guarantees and positive judicial intervention. The Supreme Court also recognised unarticulated rights that are implied by Article 21.

Public interest litigation system has been recognised in Rural Litigation and Entitlement Kendra, Dehradun vs. State of U.P.[10] (Dehradun Quarrying Case) illegal lime stone mining operations degraded the environment affecting the ecological balance in Mussoorie Dehradun area. in this case for the first time the Supreme Court held that the fundamental right to wholesome environment is a part of right to life under Article 21.

In MC Mehta vs. Union of India[11] (Ganga Pollution Case) the Supreme Court ordered for the closure of thirty tanneries of Kanpur which were releasing untreated effluents in to the river Ganges.

Closure

• Unemployment • Loss of Revenue • Loss of livelihood	• Life • Health and • Ecology

The court held that life, health and ecology have greater importance than unemployment. Right to livelihood a basic human right has been held as part of right to life by the Supreme Court in Olga Tellis[12] Case. The Supreme court was primarily concerned with the right to livelihood of the slum and pavement dwellers.

Apart from Article 21 the right to equality under Article 14 may also be infringed by government decisions that have direct impact on environment. Article 14 inter alia strikes at arbitrariness because an arbitrary action necessarily involves negating equality. Article 14 may be involved in cases where arbitrary municipal permissions were granted for constructions that are contrary to development regulations and where government sanctions for mining operations, which have high environmental impact.

Right to freedom to trade, a human right also will have reference to environmental protection. Court will have to balance environmental interests will the fundamental right to carry on any occupation, trade or business guaranteed in Article 19(1)(G). in Abhilash Textiles vs. Rajkot Municipal Corporation Gijarath High Court was required to balance the right to carry on business against the danger to public health from discharge of dirty water as to the public roads and drains.

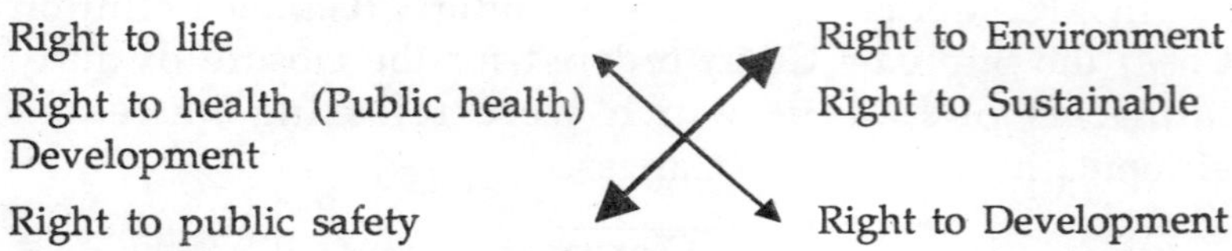

In Sardar Sarova (Narmada Project) number of human rights Vis-a-vis environment were discussed.

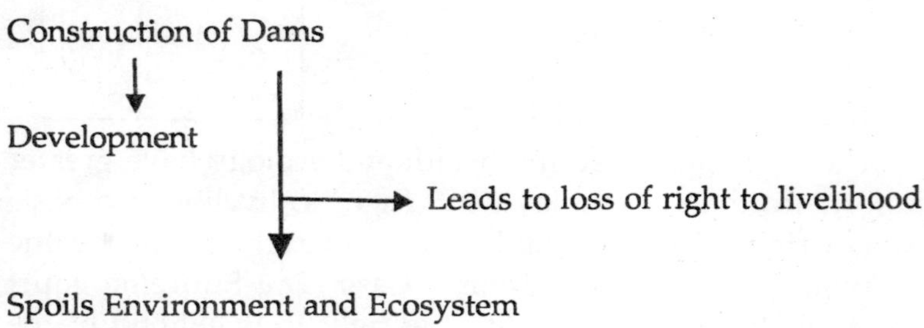

Conclusion

It is clearly reflected from the International Declarations various provisions of the Indian Constitution that law makes always wanted to give its people a clean environment so that they could live decently and happily with health, safety and dignity. In Bandhu Mukthi Morcha vs. Union of India [13] justice Bhagwati stated that right to life with human dignity enshrined in Article 21 derives its life breath from the Directive Principles of State Policy' healthy environment is also one of the Principles of State Policy hence it is covered by Article 21 which is a fundamental right.

The discussion reveals that at times it is becoming very difficult to balance the conflicting interests relating to the environment and basic human rights like life and livelihood though right to environment is also a basic human right. Again we are at cross roads to decide which is to be given priority in matters of right to life-right to livelihood, health, safety, environment and development.

REFERENCES

1. Universal Declaration of Human Rights
2. Indian Constitution
3. All India Reporters
4. Chandrapal-Environmental Pollution and Development, 1999
5. Encyclopaedia of Environmental Pollution and Control, Vol. 2, 995

1. Article 3 of Universal Declaration of Human Rights
2. Article 25(1) of the Universal Declaration of Human Rights
3. Constitution (Forty Second Amendment) Act, 1976
4. Article 21 of India Constitution
5. Article 47, 48-A 49
6. Article 51-A(g)
7. 'No person shall be deprived of his life and personal liberty except according to the procedure established by law'.
8. AIR 1978 SC 597
9. M.C. Mehta vs. Union of India (1986) 2 SCC, 176 (Delhi Oleum Gas Leakage case)
10. AIR 1988 2187
11. AIR 1988 SC 1037
12. AIR 1986 SC 180
13. AIR 1984 SC 802

13

The Rights and Responsibilities of the Elderly

Prof. P.V. Ramamurti

Based on the UN declaration of Human Rights, the International Federation on Ageing formulated a set of right for the elderly. In addition to the rights of the elderly as set of responsibilities were also formulated for the elderly. These pertain to their basic needs, living conditions, health, education and community life that are necessary to be ensured if the elder are to be considered as part of the human mainstream. In turn a number of duties or obligations have also been listed which the elderly are expected to observe, to take better care of themselves ad contribute to social, community life and national development. They are self explanatory and are listed below. It is necessary that this information is wifely disseminated not only among the elderly but also those of other age groups so it may promote a better appreciation of the privileges and responsibilities of the senior citizens.

Rights of Older Persons

1. To obtain adequate food, water, shelter, clothing and health care through the provision of income, family and community support and self-help.

2. To work and to pursue other income-generating opportunities with no barriers based on age.
3. To retire and participate in determining when and at what pace withdrawal from the labour force takes place.
4. To access educational and training programs to enhance literacy, facilitate employment, and permit informed planning and decision-making.
5. To live in environments that are safe and adaptable to personal preferences and changing capacities.
6. To reside at home for as long as possible.

Participation

7. To remain integrated and participate actively in society, and the formulation and implementation of policies which directly affect their well-being.
8. To share their knowledge, skills, values and life experience with younger generations.
9. To seek and develop opportunities for service to the community and to serve as volunteers in positions appropriate to their interests and capabilities.
10. To form movements or associations of the elderly.

Care

11. To benefit from family support and care consistent with the well-being of the family.
12. To obtain health care in order to maintain or regain the optimum level of physical, mental and emotional well-being and to prevent or delay the onset of illness.
13. To access social and legal services to enhance capacity for autonomy and provide protection and care.

14. To utilize appropriate levels of institutional care which provide protection, rehabilitation and social and mental stimulation in a humane and secure environment.

Self-Fulfilment

15. To exercise human rights and fundamental freedoms when residing in any shelter, care and treatment facility, including full respect for their dignity, beliefs, needs, and privacy and for the right to make decisions about their care and quality of life.

16. To pursue opportunities for the full development of their potential.

17. To access educational, cultural, spiritual, and recreational resources of society.

Dignity

18. To be treated fairly regardless of age, gender, racial or ethnic background, disability or other status, and to be valued independently of their economic contributions.

19. To live in dignity and security and to be free of exploitation and physical or mental abuse.

20. To exercise personal autonomy in health care decision-making, including the right to die with dignity by assenting to or rejecting treatments designed solely to prolong life.

Responsibilities of Older Persons

1. To remain active, capable, self-reliant and useful.

2. To learn and apply sound principles of physical and mental health to their own lives.

3. To take advantage of literacy training.

4. To plan and prepare for old age and retirement.
5. To update their knowledge and skills, as needed, to enhance the employability if labour force participation is desired.
6. To be flexible, together with other family members, in adjusting to the demands of changing relationships.
7. To share knowledge, skills, experience and values with younger generations.
8. To participate in the civic life of their society.
9. To seek and develop potential avenues of service to the community.
10. To make informed decisions about their health care and to make decisions about terminal care known to their physician and family.

The foregoing list of rights and responsibilities of senior citizens gives the impression that it is a tall order. They are exceedingly nice to read and fill the heart and mind of the senior citizens with mirth and self-regard. They ensure a dignified decent position for the elderly in the mainstream of human kind but alas! They only look exceedingly good in print but not in real mundane life in which most elderly steeped in poverty, illiteracy and ill health remain. For these people, the guarantee of human rights look like a pipe dream, a world of imagination far removed from the stank reality that is life. The National policy for older persons promulgated by the Government of India has, in one form or another, incorporated many of these as *desirable* provisions for the elderly. The plan of action has entrusted them to the concerned Ministries for implementation. Whether they will remain as cherished memories decorating the pages in which they are written or atleast a part of it will see the light of the day is a moot proposition.

REFERENCES

1. Andrews, G.R. (2001). Draft Research Agenda on Ageing for the 21st century, United Nations Dept. of Social and Economic Affairs, New York.

2. Gokhale, S.D. et. al. (1997). Ageing in India, Mumbai: Somaiya Pubs. Pvt. Ltd., 205-215.

3. SAARC Report (2001). Proc. of SAARC Consultation, IFA, Pune.

4. Jamuna, D. (1999). Elder care in India. Conflicting Tradition and Modernisation. In Aging Societies in a New Millenium. Proc. of 3rd International Conference of JAHSA, Honolulu, Hawaii, 33-35.

5. Ramamurti, P.V. (1995). Essentials of a Policy for the Elderly. In Vijaya Kumar (ed.) Challenges Before the Elderly: An Indian Scenario. New Delhi: M.D. pubs., 217-225.

6. Ramamurti, P.V. and Jamuna, D. (200020. Ageing in Developing Countries: The Asian Perspective. in S.D. Gokhale and Nirmala Pandit (ed.) Ageing in search of its identity, Pune: Ameya Prakashan., 277-288.

Part—III

GLOBALISATION; STATE AND HUMAN RIGHTS

14

Globalisation State and Human Rights

Prof. S. Seshaiah

This paper is about the impact of globalisation on the nature and role of the state and its capacity to protect, promote and enforce human rights. Globalisation has different meanings to different persons. There are person who believes that globalisation is the pill for every ill in the economy. There are people who have been opposing it tooth and nail and criticize that it is responsible for all evils in the economy. Some argue that globalisation is an ideology of development of present day capitalism sponsored or sold by the elite of the developed countries to the third world countries. But the 1997 Copenhagen seminar for social progress makes a useful distinction between gloablisation as a 'stage' in the historical evolution of humanity and globalisation as political 'project'. The distinction pointed out by the Coperhagen seminar provides a clue to understand the impact of globalisation on the nation-states and the so-called 'sovereignty' of third world countries. The summit calling gloablisation as a trend is to suggest that the narrowing of physical distance between people and the growing interdependence of countries represent with an unstoppable course of history, moved essentially by the application of human reason to the development of science and technology, and a general direction of change that can be capitalism or the application of the ideas and institutions of the market economy to the world as a whole. It is activity pursued by the United States and a number of other governments, from large and small countries, by the most powerful international organisations like WB, IMF and W.T.O. and financial elites. Quite naturally the prepopoments of global capitalism, presenting the free circulation of goods, services and capital a natural stage of human evolution. On the other hand the opponents of global capitalism will be inclined to play down the forces of the trend and to emphasise the decisions taken by the transnational corporations and governments favoruable to global markets.

The distinction between the 'trend' and project is however, necessary to create space for human thinking and action. With out it the 'end of history would be accompanied by the 'end of politics'. Of course, enforcement and enjoyment of rights in the ultimate analysis is politics. The inference is that there would be only one polity, one form of political organisation but serving the interest of global capitalism and leaving governments with little room for manoevuison. This process is reflecting in the thinking of elites that there is no other alternative (TNA) to globalisation. The market is everything and the state just a facilitator. As Philph Mc Michael argue that the world is on the threshold of a major political transition in the political regulation of economic activity from primarily national to a primarily global form of regulation.

Under the presence of multilateral agencies, global firms and global and regional free trade agreements, nation states increasingly surrender the organisational and ideological initiative to transnational forces. In short, he says that, nation states face a form of colonisation distinct from the colonisation of territories and people as in the past, it is a lionisation of the regulators (state actors, agencies instrumentalities) territories and peoples. Thus the transnational corporations with the help of WB, IMF and W.T.O. will encroach into the domain of state and civil society by adjusting or mending the social arrangements and institutions according to tis ideological framework. One could say that structural adjustment programmes in India or elsewhere is devices to dismantle the institutional support for the rights and their enforcement. Globalisation is the process of new colonisation of the third world countries.

"Retreat of the State"

One of the consequences of globalisation or structural adjustment programme is the change in the nature and functions of the state. A new global constitutionalism has been brought in mainly through the W.T.O. "we are no longer writing the rules of interaction among separate national formal economies. We are writing the constitution of a single world economy." (Renato Ruggerio, Director General of W.T.O.). There is no reference to governments or people here. The new constitutionalism is imposed through binding multilateral instruments of the GATT, TRIPS and TRIMS agreement that operate under the umbrella of W.T.O. with their own enforcement mechanisms. Almost all contain a pre-commitment strategy that binds future governments to certain predetermined institutional forms and policies. They counter privileged rights of citizenship on corporate capital, while constraining the power of the notion state and democratic rights of the citizen. The rules and regulations presented by the W.T.O. will directly conflict with national laws. For example, the Indian patents law and also the Indian constitution. The structural adjustment programmes, accommodated by India and implemented in the name of New Economic policies which are popularly called as liberalisation, privatisation and globalisation (LPG), stands in contradiction to the fundamental rights and directive principles of the state policies (Democratic rights).

W.T.O. is rapidly usurping the role of a global government representing the rules—based regime of the policy of economic globalisation. It seeks to remove any obstacles in the path of operations and expansion of global business interests. In practice these 'obstacles' are usually policies or democratic processes that act on behalf of working people, labour rights, consumer rights, Human rights, environmental protection, social justice, local culture and national sovereignty. A standard argument of the government and the elite is that the rigidity of labour laws allows no freedom to capital and flexibility of labour. The obstacles or impediments for structural adjustments must be removed by overhauling labour legislation. However, the legitimacy of the W.T.O. was questioned inside, by several states and outside by trade unions and people organisation at Seattle. Now the cutesy "world is not for sale".

As stated earlier that the institution most directly affected by globalisation is the state. The current restructuring of states proceeds via limitation of democratic politics, declining economic sovereignty and enslavement of state administrators in the service of global circuits. In this sense the states increasingly assume, albeit unevenly or incompletely the colonial posture administering, the coloniser's needs by organizing the exploitation of labour and natural resources for global banks and corporations. The role of government is progressively shifting towards providing an appropriate enabling environment for private enterprise. It becomes a 'transmitory' belt of global capital.

There is also a shift in the role of the state particularly in commitment to the people. There is a major change in the paradigm of state intervention, a fundamental change in its welfare and developmental commitment. After having demolished the welfare state, globalizes now speak of 'compassionate state' and human state. Jan Aart Scholate says. that, while the state has retained pivotal significance in globalising capitalism, it has lost its former core attribute of sovereignty.

The famous 'retreat of the state' is a retreat mainly from the realm of welfare and social entitlements, combined however, with very aggressive interventions in favour of capital. There has been a clear shift in the discourse of democracy and human Rights. Now democracy is the mechanism that will enable the smooth functioning of the market. The traditional values of democracy such as human dignity, freedom equality and justice are ignored. Democracy is for liberalisation and tis development model is a part of the larger agenda of gloablisation. It is a democracy tailored to suit the needs of the market economy.

Globalisation and Human Rights

The impact of globalisation on human rights is both conceptual and practical and mainly brought into focus by the changes in the nature of the state and interstate system. It is the state, which is the guarantor of human rights. It has to codify and implement human rights for its citizens. Therefore any change in the nature of state or its authority directly affects its capacity for implementation of human rights.

A global regime with an economic model that reduces the role of the state and makes it a vehicle for the market has serious implications especially for economic and social rights seen against the background of traditional second class treatment for there rights. They are in real danger of loosing their right to be rights. In spite of the affirmations of universality, indivisibility and interrelationship from the beginning, the UN itself has treated civil and political rights at one level and social and economic rights at another and apparently lower Level. There is a difference in the language of the covenants with regard to the description of rights. The International Covenant on Civil and Political rights (ICCPR), closely following the language of the universal declaration of Human Rights declares' every one has the right'. Instead, the International Covenant on Economic. Social and Cultural rights say, "State parties recognise the right of every one". It also says that the implementations of these rights are the subject to the "availability of resources". The end of the cold war gave the west a new opportunity to reinforce the claim of the primacy of civil and political rights. But there rights are also under threat from globalisation. As for economic and social rights the states can now plead non-availability of resources, as under globalisation the market deals with economic resources.

Another implication for human rights is the use of force by the state to protect 'law and order' in the interest of capital and transnational corporation and to create and maintain a climate favourable for investment. There instances officially sanctioned armed forces has been deployed against opposition to structural adjustment programmes (e.g. Venezuela and Zambia). The state, which retreats from the interest of the people, moves forward to protect the interest of the global market. The change in the nature and role of the state from 'social justice' state to 'law and order state' cause greater threat to the human rights.

15

Globalisation, Myth and Reality of Human Rights in India

Prof. (Dr.) Ranbir Singh

Globalisation though a catchword of new millennium, what is especially disturbing is the discovery of a dangerous trend in the inequality; the increasing hiatus between the urban and the rural areas. In fact, the bank report on "attacking poverty" quotes National Account Statistics (NAS) to argue that the signs of rising inequality is mainly due to rising average consumption in the urban areas but not in the rural areas. This surely provides credibility to the argument that modern development has led to the emergence of two India: the rural versus the urban, the poor versus the rich. The kisan leader Sharad Joshi had aptly described it as bharat versus India. The one time rhetoric has today uncomfortably been proved true. What are then the lessons to be learnt from such a revelation? First, with two-thirds of the population still cotnainuing to take out a living from agriculture even after half a century of independence and given a slower rate of poverty reduction in the rural areas, the task of poverty alleviation is surely gigantic. We need to go on a war footing to tackle endemic poverty in the rural areas.

The fact that a rising trend in economic growth, in the short-term, leads to increasing inequality, is an old hat. After all, it is common knowledge that a boom in the markets generates wealth, not equity and redistribution. Attempting to achieve greater equality even in classical political economy was supposed to be a function of state intervention. What is, however, surprising is that today even the market-friendly World Bank admits it. The Bank's world development report 2000-2001, notes that while India's gross domestic product (GDP) grew in the 1990s by 6.1 per cent, the decline in poverty levels has been rather sluggish. In fact, the bank recommends a comprehensive and direct approach involving "opportunity, empoverment and security." This would certainly come as a big blow for those who still continue to believe in the wonder of 'trickle-down economics.'

As a necessary fall out of trend of globalisation and liberal economic policies, India too has moved form is "Socialistic Pattern" stance to the "free market economy" with a distant shirt in the role of the state in the emerging economic order. India's new economic policy is based on the notion that economic growth is possible only if the internal entrepreneurs are liberated from state controls so that Foreign investors in India help this goal. The Government is promising attractive returns for the investment from Indian and foreign businessmen. For instance, the government has introduced or likely to introduce cuts in governmental expenditure on development as well as mass welfare schemes such as basic health care, education, subsidies on fertilizers and other welfare measures. On the other hand, various concessions and incentives are being offered to enlarge the capacities of private and foreign enterprises to invest in India on soft terms with very few or no regreatis strigns at all.

The developing countries, like India, are likely to face new challenges for the world trading system after coming into force of World Trade Organisation (WTO). Insistence of some developed countries on making environmental and labour standards as a precondition to market access and free trade would have a far reaching consequences for developing economies. The million dollar question is. Will the developing economies be able to claim an equitable share of the new world trade over. How to cope with the adverse effect of preferential trading arrangements and growing regionalism despite WTO's guiding principle of non-discrimination? What strategic laws and policies should be evolved to meet the challenge of the new world trade over?

It is worth pondering that the enforcement of labour standards will include the entire gamut of worker's rights such as freedom of association, acceptable standards of work, the rights of the migrants and immigrants and enforcement of ban on child labour, bonded labour and prison labour. Can these standards be truly enforced in our country with a liberal foreign investment regime? It is true that free market forces will further reduce the overwhelming majority of the rural poor into agrarian serfs, bonded and child labour, unemployed citizens and marginal farmers? By and large, the experience of countries that have gone through the process of restructuring the privatising their economies has been a negative one. This is true that this economic model has contributed to increased inequalities, dismantling of social services with adverse effects on the poor and restrictions on trade union rights? The development projects have negative impact on the local population, particularly indigenous people. India, which has launched the liberalisation process will be an interesting case—study to watch, whether the system would be able to protect human rights or sacrifice them for the sake of the new economic model. India forces an uphill task and a great challenge in the fiscal reform regime. One may ask: Will India's economy continue to remain stuck-up in the mess of stagflation? Who will be the ultimate beneficiary of economic growth? We also need to analyse the economic management policies with structural adjustments so as to evolve a paradigm of "socially responsible market economy". This would require proposals for reform in existing legal and economic institutions and also an examination of the social meaning of various judicial decisions creating a new regime of human rights. In other words, the glib talk among vested interests and official propagandists promising economic growth through free market economy has to be judged in terms not merely economic but social particularly when the preamble to the constitution ensures justice, social, economic and political to "We the people of India".

Second, a precondition for a successful democracy, according to the noted political sociologist Barrington Moore, has been a successful alliance between the urban middle classes and the rural peasantry. This cannot come about if the few cities continue to prosper while the millions of villages suffer. Finally, if poverty reduction became sluggish during the 1990s where the reform years, such a discovery would immediately lead those against reforms to argue: "I told you so." But on careful consideration it will be abundantly clear that one cannot blame the reforms for the slow process of poverty alleviation, especially in the rural areas. The markets have indeed performed. Consider the following: India in the '90s have moved much beyond the sluggish Hindu rate of growth: today the World bank admits that India is the fourth largest economy in the world going by purchasing power parity estimates. but why does India continue to house the world's largest poor? The state is the real culprit. Instead of ivnesting in education, public health and empowering the poor by rebuilding their entitlement, the state continued to regulate and throttle the markets for the first four decades. Today, instead of planning out the strategies of long-term poverty alleviation, it has even abandoned the basic of governance. (The Indian Express, Sept. 13, 2000).

India with the freedom history of 54 years behind is a peculiar story. Today India is free, Indians are not. Ours is a story of Republican India betrayed, promises unkept, unfulfilled and the Indian Democracy hijacked. The manifesto of the people of India provided in the preamble of the constitution, *justice social, economic, political* still remains a distant dream. The big question is what we have achieved provided in the preamble. The answer is a big no. Why this has happened? Answer is not very difficult to find, in more than five decades of freedom. India is not one India. It is two Indias. One is *"We the People of India"* that is those people who are *rich, wealthy* and *powerful* and the other category is *"We the Other people of India"* those who are *poor, downtrodden, dalits, Harijans, havenots, disadvantaged* etc., etc., sections of society. Frankly speaking the 4th World within the 3rd World. Why this has happened when the present day India has covered a long journey of freedom things has not changed much. Instead of *White Britishers* we have bred *White Indians*. The petty Indian, the havenots, have not only remained invisible to affluent eye but also feel distanced from the democratic agenda of the Indian Republic. This has happened not without a reason in all these years though the Britishers have gone, the masters have changed in place of Britishers we have Indian masters but the system remains the same it has not changed. It would be everybody's wish in the free India in the 21st century to atleast if not achieved, aspire to have some fruits of what is provided in the preamble of India which in human rights terms we call "First Generation Human Rights". The fundamental rights provided in the constitution of India and the promises of Human Rights would mean something real to all Indian if the system would respond positively to the demands of the needy, the neglected, the hapless women and the bonded child etc. The problem is not that we do not have enough laws or we are not aware of the human rights. The problem is because of the insensitivity of the people those who matter in the system. The difficulty is also of the right attitude towards the problems. Of the 80% India agriculturally based dependent on labour living in the countryside mostly without enjoying and facilities worthy name may it be proper food, shelter, clothing, health care or even education. The myth of the human rights comes more apparently visible in India and threatens to pose a much bigger problem in the new millennium. The starvation deaths are still a reality not only in Kalahandi (Orissa) but in various other parts of the country. The suicides of farmers have become common feature. The situation is really grim and explosive. It is not that we do not have enough, we have enough but not to share. I quote:

> "The fields are fruitful, and starving men moved on the roads. The granaries were full and the children of the poor grew up rachitic, and pustules of pellagra swelled on their side. The great companies did not know that the line between hunger an anger is a thin line."

If the implementation of the human rights in India have to be properly effectuated and implemented the reality of violation of human rights has to be faced with a much more sense of sincerity and honesty towards the other people of India. Otherwise what is engraved in the constitution in the chapters thereon fundamental rights and directive principles will always remain a distant dream to achieve. La would become a teasing illusion and in a state of suspended animation. One may ask how long. Nobody knows except the power that be. But the time to face the problem squately is today not tomorrow. Because tomorrow may be too late. I conclude by a conversation between Tagore and Gandhi.

Once Gurudev Rabindranath Tagore asked Gandhiji, "Gandhiji, are you so unromatic? When in the early dawn, the morning sun rises, does it not fill your heart with joy to see its reddish glow? When the birds sing, does not your heart thrill with its divine music? When the rose opens its petals and blooms in the garden, does its sight not bring cheer to your heart?"

The Mahatma Gandhi replied "Gurudev, I am not dumb or insensitive, as not to be moved by the beauty of the rose or the morning rays of the sun or the divine music of the birds. But what can I do? My one desire, my one anxiety, my one ambition is when shall I see the red tint of the rose on the cheeks of hungry naked millions of the people? When shall I hear the sweet and melodious song of the birds in place of their agonising sights? When will such music come out of their soul and when will that day come when the light of the morning sun will illumine the heart of the common man of India? When will I see its luster and brightness on his face?

We have miles to go before we sleep to realise the dream of Gandhiji. It should not be forgotten that the people of India and their human rights must have a priority in 21st century if the system has to survive the shock.

16

Right to Development and Globalisation—Paradigm

Prof. P. Prasad

The Right to development encompasses the human right associated with the process of economic, social, cultural and political development realising the fundamental freedoms to the fullest extent with entitlement for all people to effectively participate in, contribute and enjoy the benefits of that process of development. The materialisation of the development process achieving the process of growth without breaking the structures of the prevalence of a dual economy with the attendant increased inequalities and disparities and rising concentrations of wealth and economic power, and without any improvement in indicators of social development education, health care gender balance and environmental protection and violation of civil and political rights and that of the entitlement. The Right to development has been envisaged as a process of development that culminates in a process of constant improvement of the well being of the people with an active participation in development, involving in a four distribution of the benefits accruing thereof. Moreover, the right to development is considered in terms of an improvement of a vector of human rights that are interdependent together with the growth of GDP and other financial, technical and institutional resources in a manner that enables any improvement in the well being of the total population and the realisation of the sustenance of these rights along with the process of sustained development.

Development economists have conceived that development can be attained by realising economic growth and development policy is concerned with measures to rise the rate of economic growth. Development economists have opined (W.A. Lewis) that growth of output per head gives individual greater control over his environment and thereby increases his freedom, whereas some others (Kuznets) postulated that income growth and income equality are negatively correlated while emphasising the equity domain. The theories of market equilibrium in a neo classical framework have also indicated conditionary policy interactions may not reduce the efficiency of competitive equilibrium. Equity concerns were confined to certain measures that are supplementary to the policies adopted for accelerating economic growth. The human development approach (UNDP (HRDS)) brought a paradigmatic shift stressing on the expansion of capabilities and freedoms of individuals (Amartya Sen), specific policies have to be designed to extend human development approach (HRD 2000) contemplates to realise individual freedoms by enhacing there capabilities and construe this as the fundamental goal of development policy. The capabilities in turn depend on the conduct of the state and other agents and the policies that are pursued and the consequent spectrum of domain of capabilities and freedom that emerge. The design and the implementation of development policies and projects have to be in such away that they lead to higher scenarios of development along with the policies of good governance transparency and accountability along, with non discrimination, full participation and the equity maintenance in the decision making and that of sharing of the benefits. This require that the state in cooperation with the international organisations/agencies has to implement programmes aimed at improving the standard of living, access to basic resources, education, health, food, housing and other social services and employment. The developmental programmes have to provide equality of opportunity to all to enjoy the benefits and do not result in an unfair distribution of income. Further policies aimed at rising GDP should be complemented by other policies for raising human development i.e. the right to development have to facilitate the growth of resources including GDP technology and institutions. The realisation of development requires that the state should go inform legislation and constitutional changes, develop the institutions, and implement those projects for facilitating the capabilities providing stimulus to the NGO's following the holistic approach to development to ensure participation, empowerment and that of the equality. Greater international interactions are also contemplated to facilitate a higher level of international co-operation in achieving proper flows of foreign direct investments technologies, access to information and markets and that of trade and financial institutions and the emergence of new international mechanisms for catering to the specific requirements of development countries are required to facilitate the sustence of development through the enhancement of capabilities participation, entitlements and empowerment to achieve proper social and human development.

Globalisation process has been pursued in order to materialise the integration of the world/global economy inorder to reap the advantages of sustained increase in trade, investment, financial flows through the production networks carried out by the multinational and that of the giant industrial organisations utilising the information technology and the dissemination thereof. The process of globalisation envisages a higher growth of Trade in commodities and services, international financial transactions facilitating foreign direct investment and internationalisation of production, networks, markets and diffusion of knowledge and technologies with increased communication and transport network supplemented by the development of E-commerce and Trade through the vast changes in the information technology. The process of globalisation has been developing pressure on the Industrial enterprises to develop competition, exploit new markets and to go in for innovative technologies effecting to realise better quality of product and services enlarging the volume of production adopting cost effectiveness to meet the increasingly changing consumer preferences and choices. To sustain this there has been rapid shift towards market oriented policies wherein the profit motive and the price of mechanism determines the allocation of resources the developing economies have pursued Economic liberalisation, privatisation, liberalising the flow of foreign direct investments, deregulation of markets and adopting the policies amendable for removing the structural distortions to achieve the sustained increase in the process of globalisation.

Globalisation has a greater role in determining the investment levels and the patterns thereof, the structure and quality of production, prices and the opportunities for increased market access, assimilation of technologies and the involving greater international division of labour and more efficient allocation of resources thereby improving the efficiency of the economies through the increase of competition, cost effectiveness and increased market and trade opportunities through the removal of tariff barriers to Trade and vast changes in the Industrial organisations facilitated a fast expanding service sector and utilising the information flows and the economies accuring thereof. There has been a sustained increase in international Trade to world output ratio (From 12% in 1985 to 20% in 1999), foreign direct investments (US dollars 200 billion in 1990 to 885 billion in 1999). The multinational corporations were around 54 thousands with 4.9,000 affiliates in 1997 while the giant hundred multinationals account for 1/3rd of the global foreign direct investment. Trade in goods and services has increased at double the rate of global GDP while the share of the developing countries in trade has risen (to 30% in 199, as against 23% in 1985). The WTO memberships has been an increasing trend of globalisation and they are likely to continue overtime. The process of globalisation may further facilitate the integration of market of commodities, services and financial assets bringing in new global institutional frame work and medium of exchange (Euro currency and other strong currencies) increase in the arena of increased international economic dependence culminating in interactions between economic agents particularly the industry, institutions, governments and the promotional agencies to facilitate greater global co-operation and that of global prosperity to sustain economic development on mutual economic interdependence, to increase the aggregate societal welfare through the sustenance of the process of globalisation.

Economic liberalisation has been pursued through the sustenance of reforms to strengthen the management of the economy and that of the economic fundamentals for facilitating the development of a wide spectrum of economic activities, materialising competitiveness, market efficiency and considering the altered role of the state building up capability and that of effectiveness. In a transcending scenario of the global economic situation with complex economic technological and political conditions, the sustenance of economic reforms aimed to achieve economic stability and the fostering of employment opportunity through liberalisation and privatisation, in a developing economy has become difficult owing to the constraints in maintaining a non-distortionary policy environment including macro economic stability in adequate capability in investing basic social services and infrastructure and the failure in choosing effective market instruments to sustain the economic activities.

Economic liberalisation process sustained with inadequate capacity building and excessive models with inadequate investment flows and management and execution and implementation techniques of the investment of developmental projects and risk aversion attitude and behaviour prevalence could not facilitate effectively the employment generation that is required to absorb the ever increasing labour force has become a challenging and difficult task added with the complexities of problems of maintenance of economic growth efficiency and that of equity.

For accelerating the economic growth increased diversification of the economy has brought in structural changes. However, the Industrial growth materialised has been inadequate to cope with the requirements and the advantages of globalisation inspite of the pursuit of Economic reforms and that of Economic liberalisation. Higher economic growth achieved in the recent past has been more capital intensive and resulted in lower employment intensity. The trends in the annual growth of employment in the organised sector (both public and private) in the past decade (91-99) indicate that the major contribution in the overall growth of organised employment has been made by the private sectors in the post reform period whereas there was little growth of employment in the public sector. However, the growth rates of employment has not been commensurate with the requirements based on the growth of labour force. The estimates of poverty indicate a decline in the poverty ratio though the number of poor remained stable over the long period (1973-83) owing to the increase in population.

The reduction of poverty in the long run require that the acceleration of economic growth has to be more employment intensive. This has to be facilitated by Re orienting the strategies of development by increasing the capability building through people's participation, involvement and commitment in promoting and sustaining the developmental programmes, accelerating the flow of investments for the social sectors development to facilitate education, health care, maintenance of nutritional standards, housing and the infrastructure development, adopting appropriate strategies for the development of micro level enterprises and the small scale industrial units, through the fastening of entrepreneurial development of programmes, Water-shed development programmes, aforestation programmes by strengthening the gross root level promotional agencies, voluntary organisations, and N.G.O.'s, and those strategies required to increase the capability and effectiveness of the sate in providing the required basic social services and infrastructure and sustaining the policies needed for protecting the most vulnerable and to sustain the economic policies with reforms to accelerate the flow of investments to enlarge the investments for developing the competitiveness through privatisation, good governance to facilitate stronger institutional capabilities to grow faster through the sustenance of economic reforms to enhance the economic activities for materialising the growth of output, productivity and that of sustained increase in employment generation, utilising the technological advancements, information flows and the network of a participatory culture to sustain economic development while promoting the human and social development, utilising the advantages of the globalisation process while sustaining the development, realising a higher level of right to development to maximize the aggregate social welfare in a developing economy.

REFERENCES

1. W.A. Lewis, *The Theory of Economic Growth,* London, Allen and unwin, 1955
2. UNDP, Human Development Report 2000, New York, Oxford University Press
3. U.N. Independent Expert on the Right to Development, UN Doc.

17

Globalisation and its Impact on Human Rights in India

Saji Thomas

The term globalisation is used to describe the private capital flow across the world by translational corporations (TNC's). It is the integration of world market for goods, services and accumulation of profits for the richest few. Though the rhetoric gives an impression of bringing together the people from every part of the world, in reality it widens the gap between the developed and developing countries and the rich and the poor in each country. Thus globalisation has become synonymous with the economic hegemony of the rich. Globalisation is projected as the great leap of mankind in its forward march from local village communities to global markets. The Government of India is convinced that engagement with the global economy is essential to India's future prosperity.

The international financial institutions controlled by the G-8 countries force the developing countries to open their national economies to serve the economic interests of the rich countries. The International Monetary Fund (IMF) conditionalities and the Structural Adjustment programme (SAP) of the World Bank forces developing countries to integrate their economies to the global market economy. The successive Central and State Governments maintain that SAP is essential to increase GDP, employment, family incomes and living standards in India. However, so far it has led to disillusionment small farmers and business are going bankrupt everywhere; their livelihoods have been destroyed. Enron, which came to India as the flagship of globalisation has gone bankrupt. Recent developments in Argentina have shown how vulnerable and volatile are the structural adjustment programme. Let us examine important institutions, which promote globalisation.

The World Bank

The World Bank provides loans to poor countries for development projects. The bank provides loans for investment projects, such as water and sanitation, natural resource management, education and health. It also lends for what it calls adjustment projects, which are to support governments undertaking policy reforms, such as improved public sector management.

The Organisation for Economic Cooperation and Development (OECD)

The OECD develops economic and social policy for its 29 members, which include the countries of North America, Europe, Japan, Korea, Australia and New Zealand. It provides economic arguments for globalisation, and the data demonstrating the positive contribution made by multinational corporations to economic development.

The World Economic Forum (WEF)

The WEF holds an annual conference in the Swiss town of Davos, where it is based, and also holds regional conferences around the world. It has no decision-making power, but many of the world's business and political leaders discuss issues of importance at WEF meetings.

The World Social Forum emerged as a counterpoint to the World Economic Forum. It represents a broad range of interests and civil society groups with the ambitious aim of rebuilding the dreams of the left in today's globalised world.

The World Trade Organisation (WTO)

WTO is an integral part of globalisation through which the rich countries control world economy and trade World Trade Organisation (WTO) came into existence on 1 January 1995 to protect the interest of the global capital. It was established to administer the rules of international trade agreed to by its 123 member countries. Most of the world's governments are signatories to the World Trade Organisation. The key difference between the WTO and the General Agreement on Tariffs and Trade (GATT), which it replaced, is that the WTO is a permanent organisation with the judicial powers to rule on the international trade disputes. The WTO also covers trade in services, whereas GATT only covered trade in goods.

The WTO's rules make it hard for a country to favour their own industry over imports from other countries. Also, the WTO rules do not allow a country to favour the imports of one country over those from another. The WTO argues that the growth of trade between countries increases the wealth of everyone. The growth of trade is helped by the lowering of barriers, such as tariffs and import quotas, which is the object of WTO agreements.

The Structure of World Trade Organisation Comprises

1. Trade Related Investment Measures (TRIMS)

TRIMS demand national treatment of TNC's and insist transnational capital should be given level playing ground with the national capital. The Government of India demanded regulatory laws MRTP (Monopoly and Restrictive

Trade Practice Act, 1973) and FERA (Foreign Exchange Regulation Act, 1973) to suit the TRIMS agreements Recently Exclusive Marketing Rights (EMR) have been granted to TNC's in India.

2. Trade Related Intellectual Property Rights (TRIPS)

TRIPS give protection to intellectual property, which covers patents, trademarks and similar rights. India Patent Act, 1970 is amended to Suit TRIPS agreement. Our Law permitted only process pattents; that means how a particular good was made. This means one could make good by another method. Now, the product itself has to be patented. The patent protection lasts for fourteen years, unlike the Indian law which give protection for 7 years. By 2005 all laws must conform to the TRIPS regime. Actually TRIPS authorizes the Government to take control over the right to biodiversity and knowledge from communities and assign them to TNC's as exclusive monopolistic rights.

3. General Agreement on Trade in Services (GATS)

The second generations of reforms in India are to cater to the GATS of WTO, GATS take ownership over water from the local and public domain to the privatized, global domains. In other words peoples resources are transformed into corporate monopolies.

4. Agreement on Agriculture (AOA)

Under the domain of WTO transnational agri-business is given special favour. AOA prescribes a model for agriculture, that is increasing agricultural production for exports and import what cannot be produced without subsidies. AOA was based on taking decision away from farming communities. Government of India has given access to multinational seed companies over agricultural resources and market in India. AOA threaten peoples right to food security. It limits Government action to ensure stability of price for farmers by encouraging export dumping (the practice of selling products in foreign countries at prices below the cost of production). Farmers grow crops not for domestic consumption but for export to the Global market.

The Impact on Human Rights Situation in India

1. *The Right to Food*

WTO Agreements, along with the Brettenwoods institution's conditionalities are deepening the poverty in India. The SAP resulting in reduction of agriculture subsidies and withdrawal of the Government from public distribution system is threatening. Food insecurity, hunger deaths and suicides due to poverty are getting common. Many farmers have committed suicides in the last 3 years.

Poverty is a major cause of food insecurity. Food Security is the access of population to sufficient food to meet their nutritional needs. Therefore, it does not concern only the production of sufficient quantities of food. A country is food secure where all the citizens have access at all times to the food required for a healthy and productive life. Therefore food security means availability and also the accessibility to food supply.

Food security has been recognised as a basic right in the Constitution of India. The Directive Principles of State Policy spell out the social obligations of the State Article 47 says that the State shall regard the raising of the level of nutrition and the standard of living of its people and the improvement of public health as among its primary duties. Thus, the Indian State is obliged to ensure food security of all its citizens. However, with the structural adjustment programme contrary policies are taking place. On the one hand the Right to Livelihood is declared as a fundamental right of the citizens, yet on the other hand, agricultural and trade policies are such that create a situation which imperils it. The export-driven agricultural production committed to liberalisation policies of the government is disastrous for the food security of the poor.

As against grain production, farmers are engineered into producing all types of crash crops with the result that millions of hectares of land is being diverted from production of food to horticultural and oilseed production. Tomatoes have replaced cereals in Punjab, sunflower has replaced stales in Karnataka, Tamilnadu and Andhra Pradesh. A large percentage of this production will go towards feeding the burgeoning food processing industry, in which mainly TNCs are involved. Even the increase in maize production is gearned towards the animal and poultry feed market largely for export. This obviously has led to the decrease in the production of food crops.[1]

The shift in agricultual production patterns with increased dependence on food imports, spells the end of food security that the country had build up to an extent. With the introduction of the SAP regime, such commercial crops were again top priority instead of food crops. Cash crops usually benefit the Governments—who go after foreign exchange that comes from selling these commodities and the TNCs trading in rubber, tobacco, cotton, tea, cocoa and other cash crops. In times of scarcity and drought, cash crops cannot be eaten. A major problem is that land reforms have failed to allocate land for food. Futhermore, most of the water resources is distributed to producing cash crops, not for irrigation of food crops. Cash crops, which are often water intensive, also exacebrate the problem of desertification that conflict with food security.[2]

2. *The Rights of Farmers*

Agriculture is the backbone of India's economy. It provides direct employment to about 70% of the country's workforce, accounts for over 30% of its Gross Domestic Product and contributes over 20% of its exports. WTO has three major implications for Agriculture. The first is its export orientation, the second is reduction or elimination of subsidies and the third Intellectual Property Rights. The WTO agreements stipulates that:

1. Subsidies to agricultural producers shall be reduced by 20% of the 1993 rates,
2. Export subsidies shall also be reduced by 36% in some cases and 24% in others.
3. Every country shall import 3% of its domestic requirements, even if it is self sufficient in food.

These clauses are obviously meant to support the global agribusiness and go against poor farmers in India. The agreements have shifted power from the States to TNC's, thus dispossessing small farmers.

The export orientation involves changeover from staple food to commercial crops. It also involves intensive use of fertilizers, irrigation and pesticides. It runs the risk of land degradation. The main rice and wheat producing countries like USA, Australia and Argentina have plenty of land, some of which they can leave fallow for some years. Most rich countries pay their farmers to leave it fallow in order to keep production down and prices stable. WTO has banned such subsidies but allows payment for environmental protection. Their farmers can thus be paid to keep their land fallow for some years, in the name of environmental protection. India does not have any land to leave fallow. So it runs the risk of damage to its land in order to divert much of it to commercial crops for export.[3]

The small farmers who were encouraged to change over to commercial crops borrowed money to buy fertilisers and pesticides. They were given low quality products. Due to unseasonable rains and many things beyond the control of small farmers, the crops failed and deep in debt, they committed suicide. These increase in export of cotton resulted in shortage of domestic supply, which culminated in the suicide of many weavers. The emphasis in producing commercial crops for international markets results in domestic food scarcity thereby to depend on food imports.

For the past 5 years increasing number of farmers committed suicide by consuming pesticides owing to crop-failure and related indebetedness. The following implications of gloablisation have directly resulted in farmers' suicides.

- Shift from traditional food crops to cash crops, which are non-sustainable and massive exploitation of land.
- Withdrawal of subsidies on electricity, fertilizers, pesticides etc.
- Due to low priority of agricultural finance by the state, the farmers had to depend on private credit on high interest rate.

3. *The Right to Work*

The worst effects of WTO Agreements are on labour and employment. The right to work have been increasingly deprived by the anti-labour clauses of WTO, thereby increasing the number of unemployed and under-employed people. Trade unions oppose globalisation, as it leads to lowering of wages and workpalce standards. Globalisation encourages the trade in goods produced in countries, which do not allow unions to defend their workers' rights. They undercut the goods produced in countries where unions do defend unions' rights. This leads to a 'race to the bottom' as the markets are won by those with the lowest standards.

4. *The Rights of Dalits*

About 70% of Dalits in rural areas are agricultural labourers. In urban areas, a large number of them work as casual labours in unorganized sectors. Globalisation destroys the livelihood of the dalits who constitute the core of landless agricultural labourers. The reduction in agricultural labour has reduced their employment. Withdrawal of State from the industrial sector spells a similar disaster for dalits as private sector is not bound by reservation policy. In the name of development they are displaced from the place they occupy. There is no proper rehabilitation of people who are evicted from mega projects. Their right to housing is affected. Access to education, health care facilities are also diminished. The Governments at the Centre and State have been reducing expenditure on social sectors such as education, health etc. and market forces have encroached upon these sectors. This will have disastrous effect on dalits. They will be denied access to higher education health etc.,

5. The Right to Environment and Bio-Diversity

Transnational Agri-business and multinational seed companies get easy access in India, which raises serious threats to the bio-diversity of our country. The Patent Act facilitates bio-piracy of TNC's in India. In 1998, Monsanto has experimented with the terminated technology in India. It kills the reproductive capacity of the plant. So the seed cannot be reproduced and the farmer has to buy it every year from the bio-technology owning company. Environmental pollution by TNC's also poses grave threat. Pesticides and chemical fertilizers have led to severe environmental pollution and contamination of ground water resulting in health hazards.

The existing rules of the World Trade Organisation do not allow countries to ban imports of goods just because their production may have damaged the environment in the country of origin. TNC's are responsible for global warming, the depletion of natural resources, the production of harmful chemical and the destruction of organic agriculture. Hence, global companies may locate polluting industries in poor countries, log tropical forests, or develop miens with inadequate controls. Global trade in toxic chemicals, nuclear materials and other products such as genetically modified foods, or endangered wildlife, including fish poses serious threat. When the National Seed Policy was relaxed to encourage the flower industry about 40 new plant diseases and pests have entered India.

6. The Right to Education

WTO agreements will have major implications in the future of higher education in India as it will be difficult to restrict foreign educational institutions. When India agrees to implement the GATS, the government would be unable to accord a differentiated treatment to Foreign Service providers by restricting.

- The number of supplies of education services in a given subject area.
- The total value of education services per sub-sector.
- The overall number of institutions in a given sub-sector or subject area.
- The number of holders of degrees or other qualification in a given sector by applying a quota system in a given subject area.
- The number of teachers in the higher education sub-sector
- The legal form of the partnership that an education service supplier may adopt to implant itself in a given market.

The share of the market held by foreign suppliers or the amount of authorized foreign investments, whether in terms of individual companies/person or with regard to the sector as a whole.[4]

Such an opening-up of the equations sector would give a free hand to a small number of transnational corporations specialising in education, who could establish subsidiaries wherever they want by using computerised, ready-made and standardised teaching modules. Such modules would be based on a single system of values and would project a single out-look as reality. The course would be run by small units of highly mobile personnel who would travel from one country to another. As already happened in other sectors, a few large companies would compete for the "education market".

Now a student in India sitting in the virtual classroom can learn from the U.S. professor on the screen about wonderful future in biogenetic engineering. With the increasing commercialisation of education, many particulars we take for granted are being threatened. Face to face contact with teachers will slowly be phased out. As education standardisation is institutionalised through international equivalency, the uniqueness of each educational institution will vanish. The most powerful cooperations and countries will control the educational agenda of the world. With corporate controlled education, the security of the educational institution will disappear as it losses out to big merger deals and high-stakes investment. Students will be paying to work for a corporation, as it or owns their educational institution. If student financial aid was challenged as an unfair government subsidy, we could see a further reduction of educational opportunity to a narrow elite or, more precisely, a stratification in which class determines what sort of training you can afford and therefore what sort of job you are qualified for. Educational system in any society foster intellectual growth and in doing so, allow for critical thinking. The WTO is undermining our very means of resistance. There will be no power base to fight from if universities become a business.[5]

Conclusion

To conclude, there is no economic justice under the globalisation regime well underway in the world. As the state retreats to give full play to the market forces, the intensity of injustice has trend acute. Actually a distorted picture of social realities has caught the mind of the people, which has led many to imagine that there is no way out or alternative. Widening income inequalities, mounting unemployment and appalling deprivations will generate social tensions and political turbulence. The really beneficial fallout of gloablisation is that the poor too are getting aware of their identities, through not of their objective conditions. Even for their simple survival more purchasing power (through more asset distribution, social security, employment, land reforms, public works programmes etc.) will have to be given to those who can demand more goods and services. IMF, World Bank and even the UN agencies concerned with policy measures are virtually unconcerned with the dangers of unfolding inequalities and deprivations. The State has to play a more responsible role along with well meaning voluntary associations. A powerful global alliance of workers/trade unions, voluntary organisations etc, can do much in countering the onslaught of globalisation and working toward an alternate social order which is a little more just and equitable.[6] Structural Adjustment Programme has brought about adverse impact and effects of globalisation can be countered only by strengthening human rights norms and institutions which protect entitlements of the people such as, right to work, right to food, right to education, right to health, right environment etc. Since Seattle, anti-globalisation movement emerged in several places around the world strengthened by human rights groups, workers, farmers, indigenous people etc. They emerge as protest against the effects of globalisation. These protest movements strengthen the struggle for human rights and just economic order.

REFERENCES

1. Vikas Adhyanan Kendra: Mortgaging People's Livelihood and Future (2001).
2. Ibid.
3. Dr. A. Srivastava and J. Chundi; Globalisation and the Indian Farmer (1999).
4. Lok Samvad; Education under WTO (2001).
5. Ibid.
6. M.A. Oommen; Economic Justice under Globalisation (2001).

18

Globalisation, Social Justice with Reference to Right to Health of Women

Dr. K. Sreenivasa Rao
& Srinivasu

Globalisation can be defined as a process that increases the opportunities for interaction between people all around the globe. This interaction can be economic as well as social, political, scientific otherwise.

Liberalisation, privatisation and new global markatisation all come under the preview of structural programme. The structural adjustment is meant as the adjust of the economic of less developmental countries to suit the changes taking place in the highly developed capitalistic countries. Structural adjustment has the following significant features:

1. Globalisation fundamentally depends up on the new information and communication technology (ICITS)
2. Globalisation is a new political phenomena touching all corners of the global society.
3. World Bank, IMF, WTO, Multilateral Agreement on Investment (MAI)< World Economic Forum

(WEF) etc. are the institutions and are the agencies of globalisation.

4. The new economic order emphasise the importance of private sector over public sector.

5. In production structure, adjustment from emphasis on capital goods production to that of consumption goods production.

6. Governments of sovereign nation states provide the authority base for legitimating the policy preferences of those directing the global economic agenda.

7. Structural adjustment affects vulnerable groups especially women, children, disadvantaged in the form of shock therapy of drastic cut in the welfare provisions, etc.

It is fundamental premise of this paper that, the contemporary direction of globalisation represent a significant threat to the goals of those concerned with human rights with special reference to right to health.

In 1948 the UDHR was adopted for the first time in history acknowledged human rights as a global responsibility. Achieving all rights for all people in all countries is the 21st century Human Rights agenda. Poverty eradication is the developmental goal to achieve social justice to all sections of the society. Then what is social security? Is it simply fulfilling the basic needs of the people, the answer has to come from the people. If we listen to the voice of the poor, then we can understand what they really want. They view, well being holistically and describe ill, being as lack of not only food but also of work through out the year, money, shelter, clothing and health care and working in often unhealthy polluted and risky environments. These are their basic survival needs as they perceive these as basic social security. These needs have to be protected and assured during the slack periods and during calamities either natural or man made. Their power to absorbs unexpected shocks are very weak and they are reacting time to such events is slow.

Social Security and Unorganised Sector

Getuvig (1992) has given a definition of social security for unorganized sectors as; "any kind of collective measures or activities designed to ensure that members of society meet their basic needs (for instance adequate nutrition, shelter, health care and clear drinking water), as well as being protected from contingencies (for in stance, illness, disability, death, unemployment, old age), to enable then to maintain as standard of living consistent with social norm.

More precisely socio-economic security may be defined as constitution measures that enhance social capabilities, ensure economic security and enable the vulnerable section of the population to survive. Thus programme for enhancing education, health and nutritional levels of the population provision of statutory social security measure to enhance the income levels of the poor through asset and employment programmes and social assistance programmes constitute the element of our concept of socio-economic security. The agents that provide such security are spread over government firms and the community. The provision of minimum levels of income constitution not only a necessity for survival but also an essential are requisite for the acquisition of education, health and nutrition that lead to enhancing of social capability as well.

Poverty eradication is major human rights challenge of 21st century. A decent study of living, adequate nutrition and health are education, decent work and protection against calamities are not just development goals-they are also human rights.

Globalisation, Social Justice with reference to Right to Health

One of the contemporary challenges of Indian constitution of law in respect of socio-economic changes is to respond to the anti constitution pulls of the structural adjustments and globalisation programmes under way and the new economic regime emerging under the supervision of WTO. This is a danger which is real and eminent not only to India but to all developing countries.

Women and Health

Women's health is inextricably linked to their social status. In many parts of the world, particularly in South Asia discrimination against women starts before birth and continuous until death. Health statistics clearly reflect gender discrimination in South Asia an estimated 208,000 women die annually due to pregnancy and birth related complications. Norms of early marriage continued to predominate and a large majority of girls become mother before the age of 20.

Women and men in South Asia are vulnerable to many preventable and curable diseases—Tuberculosis (TB), Malaria, and Hepatitis, which become life threatening when the diseases are exacerbated by lack of information, poor health facilities, and lack of sanitation facilities and safe drinking water. The burden of disease tends to be heavier for women due to bower to health facilities, social and cultural restrictions and their low socio-economic status. Often the most trivial health problems and normal processes of child baring, because cause of mortality.

Poverty is major contributing factor to the ill health and malnutrition of women, because in the traditional society of South Asia as well as other parts of the world, poverty affects women disproportionately, what ever food is available within the household tends to be distributed in such a way that a women get a smaller share. In some communities of South Asia the tradition of sequential feeding is practised i.e. male adults first, followed by male children, then female adults and finally female children such a tradition takes a heavy tone that the health of young girls. Even in families that eat together adult women often allocate the proportions of the gender bias. Lack of education access to information, cultural taboos and religious restriction are the main reasons for low contraceptive use.

Women and Children's Health in Slum Areas (Case Study)

Of the 30% living in cities, 50% live in urban slums in conditions hardly fit for animals, India's total slum population in 1991 was 46.3 million and it is likely to be 62 million by the end of the century. This would imply that nearly 7 million children under 6 year, live in urban slums. Basic amenities like housing, water, sanitation, transport, electricity have hardly been tackled. The slum study made by the present author in Tirupati town reinforces these ground realities.

The researcher in his study related empowerment of women and human rights in the Tirupati slum area found that the selected sample were victim of poor environmental conditions such as poor sanitary condition, polluted water and air and stagnate pools that breed mosquitoes. Added to that the women were subjected to poor nutrition, over work, high fertility and lack of access to reproductive health care. It was also found that the slum women are not only treated by untrained midwife but also resort to traditional medical treatments. The slum women were subject to victim of basic human rights violations. unfortunately they suffer silently and accept them as their fate. The slum women continue to live in culture of poverty. The life of slum women is caught up with problems of today and she can't think of the next day, let alone the future. She has been socialised to believe that self denial rather than self assertion is a truly feminine virtue. She is in the culture of silence and never makes an attempt to move in the culture of participation. The researcher concluded in his paper stating that slum women needs self confidence and self reliance so that the silence and invisibility surrounding their human rights violation can be arrested.

India is a pioneer in health service planning over the last 5 decades massive infrastructure manned by large number of medical and paramedical person has been created by the government, voluntary and private sectors to provide primary, secondary and territory level health care services to urban and rural population. We can truly feel proud of the steep decline in crude death rate from 25.1 in 1951 to 8.7 in 1999 and birth rate has fallen to 26.1; life expectancy rose from 32 years in 1947 to 61.1 years in 1991-96.

In spite of these achievements, however, India rates as low as 138th among 174 countries in terms of the human development index, which includes health as one of the Indicators. The morbidity due to common communicable and nutritional related disease continued to be high. Morbidity due to non-communicable disease is showing a programme increase because of increase in longevity and attractive life styles we must address these areas of concern and rapidly improve the health system of the population.

Globalisation, liberalisation and privatisation have no future, driven as they are big business which does strayed in hunger and poverty and makes money by patents on life saving drugs. How else do you explain 6,00,000 women dying each year as result of pregnancy and child birth. 99% of them in poorest countries. India motherhood tool is one death out of 37 while for China, less opulent but more concern with overall human condition, the pregnancy, maternity peril is one in 400. Neglect of investment in people and diversion of resources for fivestar culture of the creamy layer will, sooner than later developed into full-blown confrontation between the people and socialistic constitution of India on the one hand and the MNC-5th Column combined who corner wealth and aggravate the grim disparity. The article 38 of over constitution is only in theory and not in practice this is evident in the presents of acute poverty in the country the poor is becoming poorer and rich is becoming richer thanks to LPG.

The researcher in yet another study related 50 landless women agricultural labourers belonging to backward class community found that they are deprived of basic needs such as drinking water, fuel, food, shelter, clothing and health care delivery system. Poverty is the single most factor coming in their way, coupled with in the wet areas landlessness and lack of employment for about 5 months a year during slack period and in dry areas extremely low average wages below minimum prescribed by the government despite work availability throughout the year.

In terms of health care delivery system they still depend upon traditional health practices. The primary health centres are located far away from their residence and they lack basic infrastructure facilities, skilled, trained medical and paramedical personnel. This is the ground reality with regard to health of the rural dalit women. The micro study of the primary health centre given below would further reinforce our ideas with case analysis.

Right to Health at the Grassroot Level: A Micro Level Study of the Primary Health Centre, Pachikapalam of Vedurukuppam Mandal of Chittoor District

Health is a state of complete physical, mental and social well-being, and not merely an absence of disease or infirmity—World Health Organisation.

Rising the level of nutrition and standard of living and improving public health—Article 47 of the Indian Constitution.

Introduction

Health does not exist in isolation. It is influenced by a complex of social, economic, political, responsibility of the state in providing health care services are grossly neglected in many of the third world countries. In order to study, how, several factors, affect the right to health of the people, an attempt is made by taking the micro-level study of *Primary Health Centre, Pachikapalam of Vedurukuppam Mandal of Chittor District,* A.P.

Within a span of three months one patient is delivered at bus stand and another patient is died due to criminal negligence of hospital main staff. Various factors such as politisation of the institution, corruption, profit motive of doctors rather than service motive, inadequate infrastructural facilities, unhygienic environment are maladies. There inturn, result in sheer violation of the right to health of the poor. In order to remedy this situation, only the awareness of the public, along with committed progressive political leadership is suggested. The implication of violation of human rights at the grassroot level is discussed.

Case I

Irla Gopal Raju aged about 39 years belonging to Inam Kothru Village of Vedurukuppam Mandal. He was taken to P.H.C. Pachikapallam on October 9th 2000 by 3.00 p.m. with the complaint of Snake Bite. At that time the PHC is closed. The patient attendant asked for doctor. The doctor was on leave and residing at Tirupati.

After that the patient Attendant went to Staff Nurse Home and told the condition of the patient. The Staff Nurse not come to PHC immediately. She send a person to the Attender's house for PHC keys. The patient condition is very serious the attendants are crying for treatment. By 3.30 p.m. the patient was died without First Aid. The patient relatives and public was angry towards the staff due to negligency of the OP Staff the patient died. In the next day news published in VARTHA daily paper also. The medicines i.e. Anti snake venom is available in PHC. But the Medical officer or staff not available at that time. The Staff Nurse explained the PHC is closed because it is lunch break. Whatever it may be the poor person died without treatment. He has a wife and two children.

Case II

A patient by name Kali, Saroja, age about 22 years came to PHC on 7th December 2000 with labour pains. At that time the Medical officer is on tour. The Staff nurse examined the patient and refer the patient to Tirupati because due to it was I para of pregnancy. Due to the financial problem the patient not went to Tirpati immediately they are waiting for 1 hour at Bust stand. The pains came delivered a female child at Bus stand. It is due to the inefficiency of Medical Staff.

Pachikapalam is located at 30 k.m. away from Tirupati town. It is a junction for number of villages. The demographic details are provided below.

Men	22054
Women	21244
Total	43298

Here there is a Mandal Primary Health Centre, under the supervision of District Medical and Health officer, Chittoor with the following staff.

Civil Assistant Surgeon (or) Medical Officer -1

Community Health Officer	-1
Staff Nurse	-1
Lab-Technician	-1
A.N.M. (OP)	-1
Senior Assistant	-1
Pharmacist Grade-II	-1
Attender	-1
Field Staff	-1
(8-sub-centres)	-15

In adequate Infrastructure and Mismanagement

It is a 3 bedded hospital with a single doctor. No operation theatre. No Oxygen Cylinder for emergency purpose. The staff is in sufficient. If the doctor is on leave or on camp the treatment is given by para medical staff only.

This PHC covers 43298 population of the mandal. The medicines are not supplied sufficiently. Only Rs. 10,000/- medicines are supplied to the PHC per month.

Ambulance: No vehicle facility available in the emergency the patients wait hours together for bus.

Urbanisation: Majority of the medical staff residing at Tirupati because of education of their children and likes town environments. If the staff staying at their head quarters the treatment is available better to the public.

Building Facility: There is no own building to the PHC. The hospital run in the rented building with insufficient rooms and beds. If the building is constructed with quarters—the staff available for 24 hours to the public.

Politicisation: Generally in every mandal the PHC is at mandal head quarters. But here it is away 5 km to the mandal. Because some political pressures the PHC is at Pachikapallam. Now it is corner to the mandal. It cover 8 sub centres from Devalamkpeta sub centre. It is 30 km from PHC. The PHC is near to the Karvetinagar mandal.

Now the new building is constructed at T.R. Puram 1 k.m. away from Pachikapallam at Karvetinagar road. It is also inconvenient to the public, if it is near to th Bus stop then only it is convenient to the public.

Health Insurance

The privatisation of health institution would only add burden to this section of the society. With privatisation and Globalisation there is a eminent danger of a vast section of people living below poverty line loosing their very right to health care. If the health sector is privatized with out making arrangements of free or subsidized minimum health care to the poor and disabled persons the structural adjustment would only bring shock therapy to the poor. The SAP programmes is affecting the vulnerable section of the society by depriving the right to health, social justice enshrined in our constitution.

Surveys carried out NSSO indicate that high cost of hospitalisation is one of the factor leading to indebtedness especially among the low and middle income group population. Health insurance to meet the cost of hospitalisation for major illness will ensure that health care cost do not become a major financial burden or cost of indebtedness among these patients or their families. Over the past two decades several health insurance schemes have been introduced. There are individual, family or group insurance schemes for health care. Senior citizens insurance and insurance for specific disease. Appropriate mechanisms for the people of below poverty line are to be met well have to be evolved tested and implemented. The protective type programmes such as old age pensions, widow pensions, survival benefits etc., provide a certain degree financial support to poor or destitute persons facing specified adverse contingencies. Another potential advantage of protective schemes is simplicity and relatively low administrative cost if appropriately designed.

The main objective of Nation Health Policy of 2001 is to achieve an acceptable standard of good health amongst the general population of the country through universal provision of comprehensive primary health care services. The private sector will continued to play a role in provision of curative services at such a role will need to be monitor through adequate regulatory mechanisms. The NHP 2001 envisages an increased allocation 55% total public health investment for primary health sector 'The secondary and territory health sectors being targeted for 35% and 10% respectively. NHP 2001 envisages the utilisation of NGOs and civil society organisations in monitoring public health programmes and increasing participation of local communities in planning and implementation of such programmes. They would also have a major role in community mobilisation and in building the capacities of panchayat Raj institutions.

Hope with the self assertion of people especially women in the society with the support of civil society institution and NGOs at the grass root level would soon enjoy the right to health as enshrined in the UDHR, Article 25-1 and even in our constitution.

REFERENCES

1. Babu, B.V, Chhotray, G.P., Hazra, R.K. and Satyanarayana, K—Perceptions and Interactions of Vulnerable Groups with the Government Health Services. Indian Journal of Social Work, Vol. 61, (1) Jan, 2000.

2 Banu Rama, V—Private Health Care in India, Social Characteristics and Trends. Sage Publications, New Delhi, 1998.

3. Chandra, P.B., Singh and Usha Rani Singh—Health: A Human Right Issue. Journal of Social welfare, Vol. (45) No. (6), September, 1998.

4. Report of the National Health Policy-2001.

5. Rao, Mohan, (Ed) Disinvesting in Health, The World Bank's prescriptions for Health. Sage Publications, New Delhi, 1999.

6. U.N. and Health, UN Weekly Newsletter, 27 April-3 May 20001, P. 5-7.

19

Structural Adjustment—And MNC

Smt. P.B. Pankaja

Globalisation has become a subject of very serious discussion in the national economic policies. The very evolution of NEP in 1991 in India is a spontaneous response to the external shock of globalisation. The time has now crossed to debate whether the LPG model conditioned by World Bank in necessary or not. There is no escape for LDCs and developing countries from the triangular Fund-Bank package of privatisation, liberalisation and globalisation. The Structural Adjustment Programme (SAP) has become the present day way of life in Indian political economy. All our efforts should go to see how best we can pursue the SAP with less pain and more comfort.

Globalisation means adopting a global outlook for the trade and trade strategies, aimed at enhacing global competitiveness. Corporates which have adopted a global outlook stop thinking of themselves as national marketers but as global marketers who venture abroad. They establish world wide manufacturing units, make global market policies and foster global financial flow. Thus a true global corporation views the entire world as a single market as borderless economic world. The Managers of Honda and

Casio see all their customers equidistant from the corporate centre. There is nothing like home market and international market in their dictionary.

Two important factors contribute for globalisation:

(i) Pull factors such as profit and growth prospect and

(ii) Push factors such as compulsion for domestic market for globalisation. Our NEP is a reaction of the 2nd factor.

What is SAP?

The World bank and IMF popularly known as Bretton Wood Institutions assumed the role of universal guardians of a rational economic order and started playing pivotal role in the political economy of the LDCs. 'By coaxing or cajoling, browbeating or threatening'[1] they mould the opinion of the political leaders and their bureaucrats towards what they would consider as desirable policies. These package of policies intended to achieve good economics include finance and a set of conditionalities. These conditionalities become incorporated in the policy frame work paper (PFP) that defines the relationship between the BWIS and the recipient countries. Bound by PFP, the recipient countries introduce Structural Adjustment programmes in their national economics.

Thus the LPG model, i.e., the liberalisation, privatisation and gloablisation, is the brain child of BWIS and form the core of SAP. Through LPG, the national economy is expected to march towards global economic prosperity.

What is MNC?

Globalisation and multinationalism are two sides of the same coin. Multinational Corporations are a particular breed of firms, different from others, which are large, vertically integrated and whose area of operation covers many countries with their subsidiaries and affiliates and operate mostly in oligopolistic marketers. Their vastness can be measured by their annual turnover, assets, man power, R and D expenditure and control over technology. With their size and enormous economic power they have better bargaining power with the governments of LDCs. They also wield considerable political power through political contributions. They even play a key role in making and breaking governments. Their investing capacity makes it possible for them to have access to even inaccessible areas such as tundras, deserts and tropical forests. Their network in any specified field extends to chain operations beginning with exploration, development, production, transplantation, refining and marketing. These giant corporate, having both forward and backward linkages, make it extremely difficult for a new competitor to enter into the industry and survive. The existing smaller corporate are forced either to integrate themselves with these MNCs in submission or quit the market. Executives are trained in world wide operations and management is recruited from many countries. Raw materials are purchased where they can be obtained at the least cost, and investments are made where the anticipated profits are the greatest.[2]

An I.L.O. report observes, the essential nature of the M.N. enterprise lies in the fact that its managerial head quarters are located in one country—known as 'home country' while the enterprise carries out operations in a number of other countries called 'host countries'. "The economic clout of the MNC is indicated by the fact that the G.D.P. of most of the countries in smaller than the value of sales, turnover of the M.N. giants."[3]

SAP and MNCs

Thus under SAP, MNCs are given warm welcome by the LDCs and developing countries. Through liberalisation, the doors of trade are thrown open for MNCs to stretch their operations in the national economy. Suffering from financial drain, surplus human resource and poverty and induced by BWI packages, LDCs accept them as their saviours of economic crisis and contributions to their national prosperity. The MNCs in turn, attracted by the SAP, bring in Foreign Direct Investment (FDI) to these countries. These developments have naturally attracted serious controversies like.

1 Whether SAP is boon or bane to LDCs?

2. Whether MNC's entry in national economics of LDCs really destroy indigenous trade institutions?

3. Whether any safeguards available to endure the journey of SAP towards global economic prosperity, with less pain and more comfort?

Growth of MNC

In the early days, the U.S. was the home of most of the MNCs. In 1862-63, the U.S. based Singer sewing machines was the first MNC established in England. Now there are many European and Japanese MNCs. MNCs from developing countries such as S. Korea and Taiwan have also been making their presence increasingly felt. The first MNC came to India in 1921.

With the advanced stage of globalisation, large corporations known by different names such as MNCs, INCs, TNCs have become very popular driving force in the world economy. At the end of 1991, there were 245 Indian joint ventures in abroad dispersed over 43 countries and 469 foreign companies in India.

Whether MNCs are boon or bane?

As the Preface to the ILO report on Multinational Enterprises and Social Policy observes, "for some, the multinational companies are an invaluable dynamic force and instrument for wider distribution of capital, technology and employment; for others, they are monsters which our present institutions, national or international cannot adequately control, having a law to themselves with no reasonable concept, the public interest or social policy can accept."[5]

1. MNCs help in increasing the investment level and thereby the income and employment in the host country.

   Eg..: Brazil, Mexico, Singapore and South Korea.

2. They have become vehicles for transfer of technology to the developing countries.

3 They cause managerial revolution in host countries through professional and highly sophisticated management techniques.

4. They enable the host countries to improve their exports.

5. They integrate national economics wherein world's desires and needs have been irrevocably homogenised.[6]

6. Huge financial resources at the disposal of MNCs enable them to have very efficient research projects and development systems.

7. They break domestic monopolies.

However they are subject to a number of criticisms:

1. MNCs destroy local competition and monopolies and emerge as unimpeachable monarchs.

2 They may even threaten national sovereignty of host countries.

3 They overexploit the non renewable national resources of host countries.

4. Transfer pricing enables MNCs to avoid taxes by manipulating prices on intra company transactions.

5 They drain the foreign exchange resources of the host countries.

6., They tend to invest in the low priority and high project sectors, ignoring the national priorities of the host countries.

7. MNCs decide what to produce and how to produce, where to sell and at what price, ignoring local needs.

8. MNCs may deny vital information to host countries which may increase their bargaining power.

Changing trend in MNCs

Amidst criticism we also find a changing trend in MNCs.

1. The major part of the business of the MNCs was originally in the developed economies. But economic reforms like privatisation and liberalisation ushered in the LDCs due to SAP have attracted FDI by MNCs in these countries.
2. Some MNCs have accommodated themselves more to the needs of the LDCS.
3. Many more nationals like Japan and E.E.C. are now competing with U.S. MNCs.
4. Developing countries like Argentina, Brazil and Hong Kong themselves are now stabilizing multinationals.
5. LDCSs started comparing the political and economic attractions of variety of foreign companies and weighing them against their costs and paying them off against one another.
6. There is now much interest in trying to formulate I.N. codes of conduct for the MNCs. The ILO has created one such committee as a model.

7. MNCs in several developing countries made substantial contribution to export earnings.

MNCs in India

In India, due to several factors, very little foreign investment has taken place, comparatively. Some multinationals like coco cola and IBM, even left India in the date 1970s as the government conditions were less acceptable to them. Till 1980s we have consistently followed policies that favoured production for the local market than for exports. However with economic liberalisation that increased domestic competition and steady depreciation of the rupee, export became attractive. Several foreign companies and even Indian companies have become serious about exports. In an analysis[7] about the functioning of MNCs in India, it is found that several Indian outfits of MNCs like Pond's, Johnson and Johnson, Lipton, Brook Bond, Colgate-Palmolive etc, were in the low technology consumer goods sector. Hindustan Lever, while popular in the low-tech consumer goods, has diversified into high technology and export oriented sectors. Pond's had diversified into thermometers, leather upper and mushrooms entirely for exports (Pond's, Brook Bond and Lipton were merged with the parent company, Hindustan Lever) ITC (Indian Tobacco Company—formerly Imperial Tobacco Company) has diversified into areas like hotel, paperboards and edible oil. There are MNCs, like Siemens, which are in high technology areas. There are several MNCs in the pharmaceutical industry, like Glaxo, Bayer, Sandoz, and Hoechst. MNCs like Marubeni and Nissho Iwai confine to foreign trade.

It is also wrong to assume that the success of MNCs is guaranteed in developed countries and that the domestic firms will not wishstand the competition from them. The Double Cola has not been a success in India. Parle appeared to be very much worried about the entry of the Pepsi and it did every thing to prevent its entry. But, when the competition became a reality, it faced its head on and the reports are that the Parle Brands are far outselling the Pepsi's. in the soft-drink concentrate market, while Juc of the Kothari-General Foods (MNC) combine failed, the product of the small firm, Pioma industries (Rasna) has become a grand success. Asian paints which had its beginning as a small unit has become the unrivalled industry leader, successfully fighting multinationals. Similarly, the Nirma story is well known. There are several foreign brands like, Tang, which have miserably failed. Thus the general apprehension that all foreign brands will have sweeping success at the cost of Indian brands is to be analyzed in the light over circumstances.

References

1. Biplas Das Gutpa—*The New Political Economy of Development,* P. 60.

2. Phillip Kotler.

3. Francis Cherunilan., *Business Environment,* p. 571.

4. *Ibid,* p. 580.

5. *Ibid,* p. 574.

6. Theodore Levitt, *The Globalisation of Mkts,* Harward Business Review, May-June, 1983, p. 92-93.

7. Francis Cherunilam, *Business Environment,* p. 580.

20

Globalisation Reflects and Affects the Rights of Child in India

Rayadurgam Narayana

Introduction

Legal and economic systems lie intertwined within the institutional frame work of any society. Human history shows that economic environment and the corresponding legal framework have undergone drastic changes from time to time. Modern economic history begins with the emergence of capitalism. It was engendered and fostered by colonial occupation and exploitation of the rest of the world by the west during the 18th century. In its first phase, the industrial revolution and its resultant economic growth gave birth to laissex-faire capitalism. To meet its requirements, a new legal system was developed. In the beginning of the 20th century the struggle of the underprivileged masses culminated in the Bloshevik revolution in Russia. The communist system which was established after the revolution, demolished the then existing legal system and framed a new system of law to suit the communist economic philosophy. On the other hand, in the U.S.A. after 1930's Depression, the *laissez-faire* capitalism collapsed paving the way for the emergence of state controlled capitalism in its place. During this period, the entire existing legal system underwent through change to suit the new situation. In India, after independence an experiment was made with the mixed economy based on the economic philosophy of democratic socialism. During this period, the country witnessed drastic changes in the Constitution and the laws governing economic matters. The Constitution was amended many a time to tackle emerging problems. The court at first, hesitated to reconcile itself with these amendments but modified its attitude later. After 1990, gloablisation, liberalisation and privatisation brought a 'U' turn in Indian economic policy which led to wide ranging changes in industrial policy, with attendant impact on legislations and judicial attitude.

The word 'Globalisation' is now used widely to sum of today word order. It means they increasingly integrate the world into one capitalist political economy operating under a neo-liberal free market ideology. Economic globalisation as witnessed in the world today is not a new phenomenon. It has been evolving for the past several years and gaining momentum day by day. The trend, at present, is a shift from a world economy based on national market economies to a borderless global market economy increasingly governed by one set of rules. In this context, 'globalisation' means global economic liberalisation developing a global financial system and a transnational production system which is based on a homogenized world-wide low of value.

The goal of democratic socialism based on the cherished ideals of Gandhism and Marxism began to disappear with the advent of liberalisation, privatisation and globalisation. During the eighties, to grapple with the mounting economic problems several new economic models were vigorously tried but most of such experiments were not successful. Nevertheless many changes took place during the eighties and finally almost everything changed during nineties. In the process the spirit of the Constitution which supported democratic socialism was also enfeebled. Globalisation along with electronics and communciaton revolution brought drastic changes in the world economic order. Globalisation, privatisation and market friendly approach have led to several perceptible changes in the world order. Breakdown of the Communist model in Soviet Union and Eastern Europe and the resultant rise of the single polar power system under the U.S.A. and internationalisation of economic system with the aid and guidance of I.M.F., World Bank, W.T.O. conditionalities leading to the emergence of today's neo-capitalism are some of them. These factors enabled the U.S.A. and the West at attempting to mould the world economic order in their favour at the expense of poor nation.

Globalisation has substantially contributed to the synchronizing the debt, poverty and economic chaos in the developing world. The structural adjustment programmes (SAP) designed and imposed by the global creditor institutions in a typical instrument to create a favourable atmosphere for globalisation, which ultimately effects developing countries. In order to meet the mandates set by the Structural Adjustment Policies (SAP) as country spends less, by cutting back government expenditures, social services, and economic investments so that resources can be placed elsewhere. More moneys is being spent on export orientation, which results in local economies becoming dependent on the integration with the world economy. The international leaders demand poor economies to divert substantial resources away from sectors serving domestic needs, withdraw all subsidies for poor people, private the state sector, deregulate the market and decrease wages. In effect, this process opens up countries to globalisation.

Globalisation Policies how it affect the Human Rights in India

The advocates of globalisation give philosophical justifications to accept export-led growth, lower wages and living standards for workers, shrinking governmental budgets and extremely high interest rates. The developing countries are left into the option but to accept the liberalisation and market oriented reforms. Under this liberalisation policy production tends to be export-oriented. Meeting the basic needs of the people become less important. State run factories or enterprises are often privatised to suit the needs of foreign investors. Free trade, liberalisation lead to competition and local producers like farmers have to suffer the consequences.

Thus the structure, power and role of the international trade and economic organisations like IMF, IBRD, World Bank and W.T.O. which are dominated by the U.S.A. and Europe are designed assist to liberalisation, privatisation, globalisation, market friendly approach, free and protected flow of foreign capital, especially for the benefit of the rich capitalist nations. These global changes had their profound impact on India as well. Owing to this impact of globalisation, the basic economic policy is undergoing drastic changes. The first and fore most was the change in the industrial policy resolution. The entire economic laws are also undergoing changes. To cope with the directions of the above mentioned world institutions and in line with globalisation a large number of economic laws have been changed in tune with the new trend. Laws relating to regulation of foreign exchange, MRTP, Company, Arbitration, Intellectual property etc. have been changed to suit the needs of liberalisation, privatisation and globalisation. The industrial policy after the liberalisation is totally different from what it was in the past and makes no distinction between foreign investment and domestic investment.

Recent decisions of the court show that judiciary also has accepted the trend of globalisation and its socio-economic impact. The court had declared that bureaucracy should adopt a positive approach to stimulate production and productivity in every sector of economy, so as to increase the size of the national cake.

Globalisation requires the humiliation of hundreds of millions of people keeping them in constant insecurity, pitting them against one another in a competitive struggle for survival.

Even the people of developed countries suffers form the profit-hungry rules of global corporations today, which virtually rules the world. Globalisation and market-oriented economic reforms have been designed for the benefit of these groups. In reality, globalisation means the rule of global corporations. It means decision about lives are being made in corporate bed rooms in the U.S.A. Europe and Japan instead of in local community councils or at the national level.

Today the National Governments are at pivotal scenario, acting as delivery mechanism to release orders to receiving mechanism. This has created a new horizon of powerlessness, normlessness, lawlessness, anarchy. It also amounts in harassment, humiliation and violation of just rights of billions of citizens.

Human rights have become an integral part of the process of globalisation in many ways. The western countries are increasingly using their view of human rights. Concept as a yardstick to judge developing countries and to deal with economic and trade relations to expand development assistance. At the same time globalisation intensifies by increasing poverty, insecurity and fragmentation of society and thus violates human rights, human dignity of millions of people.

As a result, the process of globalisation which makes more negative effects. Global integration of the structures, processes and ideologies produce injustice, oppression, suppression, depression, exploitation and maldevelopment in society. The systematic integration of the forces that are dominant in the globalisation process intensifies human rights violations.

Role of Trade in Human Rights

The recent acceleration in the process of economic globalisation has induced widespread concern that government and labour organisations may no longer be able to preserve those 'core' labour standards. The International Labour Office (ILO) deems fundamental to human dignity In 1993 this concern led the International Confederation of Free Trade Unions (ICFTU) to call for the inclusion of a labour clause within the programme of the World Trade Organiation (WTO) that would aid the preservation of these basic rights. Though this demand has not yet been endorsed by the WTO it has won support from the Governments of North America and from the European Parliament (EU) and will be debated at the WTO's first Ministerial meeting in December 1996. The leader of the many Institutions promoting a labour clause argue that if international trade and the defence of labour standards are not linked up there may occur a global devaluation of employment conditions with nations engaging in a competitive 'race to the bottom'.

Reflects of Globalisation and how it Affects the Rights of Child

Protection of basic human rights is now recognized as a primary obligation of every society whatever its political ideology or level of development. Since word war II, the activities of liberal and democratic societies and of the United Nations and its specialised Agencies, there has been universal acceptance of minimum human rights standards usually protected by the constitution and the laws of various countries. Due to Liberalisation, Privatisation, Globalisation (LPG) policies in India arbitrary exercise of power, denial of equality, justice and human dignity have been fought by individuals and groups through legal and political processes in the country.

Globalisation is a symbol of economic access to the whole globe without tariff restrictions, administrative ban or other legal bar. However in India the indiscriminate opening up of the economy to foreign investment almost in every sector has reduced the essence of fundamental rights offered to citizens under Part III of the Constitution. Art. 19(1)(g) offers the right to practise any profession or carry on any trade or business to citizens. But the reforms introduced in tune with globalisation now equally protect the rights of foreign investors as well. Almost all economic laws give equal protection of foreigners because of internationalism of such trade and commerce. However, Art. 19(1)(g) remains the same and its protection still is not extended to non-citizens.

The new economic policy and legal reforms totally negate the implementation of programme under Article 38 and 39. Equitable distribution of material resources of the community for the common good and prevention of concentration of wealth and income are the basic dreams of the framers of the Constitution. They have now become mere mirages for the vast majority of common people of the nation. The court also opined that the Constitution adopted mixed economy, and control over the industry in this estáblishment, working and production of goods and services. But after recent liberalisation of the free economy, private and multinational entrepreneurship has gained ascendancy and entrance into wider commercial production and services, domestic consumption of goods and large scale industrial productions. Even some of the public cooperation are thrown open to the private national and multinational investments. It is axiomatic, whether or not industry controlled by Government or public corporations would also be subjects to the same Constitution limitation in the trinity viz, Preamble, Fundamental Rights and Directive Principles.

Art. 46 requires special care by State in education and economic advancement of weaker sections. Art. 39(a) is for the introduction of all legal system to promote justice to all. Art. 16(4) enjoins on the State to make special provisions for the reservation of public employment in favour of backward classes of citizens who are not adequately represented in the service of the state. In the present era of liberalisation, privatisation and globalisation, public employments are substantially reduced. In such a situation, it may not be possible to offer public employments are substantially reduced. in such a situation, it may not be possible to offer public employment to many. Public sector and governmental activities become lesser and lesser because of the policy of disinvestment and privatisation leading to shrinking of public employment opportunities at an alarming rate. Indeed there would be consequent increase in private employment. But the protections afforded by fundamental rights in he area of public employment will not be available in the private employment sector. Thus the economic protections guaranteed by fundamental rights and directive principles in the area of public employment will be deprived to a vast majority of people. Similar is the case with regard to the protection guaranteed under Art. 16(4) which offers reservation in public employment for socially and educationally backward classes. The same is the fate of Scheduled Caste and Scheduled Tribe. The grand vision embodied in the Preamble with regard to social and economic justice now slowly vanished.

Viewed from this angle, a new trend in our society is the emergence idea of "Children's Rights" within the context of human rights. These claims, made on behalf of the children include a right to be protected from the influence of religion; a right to choose their own home, their school and their friends, freedom from restraint and punishment, a right to love and happiness, a right to a better life for handicapped children, a right to sexual education, a right to a new democracy in education, freedom from being indoctrinated; freedom to have compulsory education; a right to be educated without any form of let or hindrance devised by adults, a right to be educated for a job and to cap it all, treated as the 'Rights of Children'.

Our Constitution makers, wise and sagacious as they were, had known that the India of their vision would not be a reality if the children of the country are not nurtured and educated. For this, their exploitation by different profit makers for their personal gain had to be first indicted. It is this need, which has found manifestation in Article 24, which is one of the two provisions in part III of our Constitution on the fundamental right against exploitation. The farmers were aware that this prohibition alone would not permit the child to contribute its mite to the nation building work unless it receive at least basic education. Article 45 was therefore inserted in our paramount parchment casting a duty on the state to endeavour to provide free and compulsory education to children. This provision in part IV of our constitution has after the decision by a Constitution bench of this court in Unni Krishnan, J.P. vs. State of A.P., (1993) ISCC 645, acquired the status of a fundamental right...'

For the protection and development of the children, India adopted policies, convention, convenants and also enacted several laws.

For Example

- The National Policy for Chidren in 1974
- World Summit for Children, 2000
- Government of India's National Nutrition Policy—1993

- The Integrated Child Development Services (ICDS) 1975
- The National Policy on Education—1986 and also Education for all—2000
- Universal Immunisation Programme, (Pulse Polio)
- Universalisation of Primary Education and eradication of illiteracy in the age group of 15 to 35 years are the basic objective of 8th five year plan i.e. (1992-1997)
- Children in difficult circumstances
- Government of India National Plan of Action on Commitment to the Child—1992

These are all policies, programmes especially to promote the cause of children in India. Apart from this there are four sets of civil, political, social, economic and cultural rights of every child according to convention on the Rights of Child, 1989.

1. **The Right to Survival,** Which includes the right to life, the highest attainable standard of health nutrition and adequate standard of living.
2. **The Right to Protection,** which includes freedom from all forms of exploitation, abuse, inhuman or degrading treatment, right to special protection in situations of emergency and armed conflicts.
3. **The Right to Development,** which includes the right to education support for early childhood development and care social security, leisure, recreation and cultural activities.
4. **The Right to Participation,** which includes respect for the views of child freedom of expression, information freedom of thought, conscience and religion.

The state shall direct its policy towards securing the health and strength of workers men and women and the tender age of children are not abused. The children are given opportunities and facilities to develop in a health manner and in conditions of freedom, dignity and that youth and childhood are protected against exploitation and against moral and material abandonment.

'Despite the above, the stark reality is that in our country like many others, children are exploited lot, Child labour is a big problem and has remained intractable even after about 53 years our having become independent and despite various legislative enactments.

Based on the facts reveal that inspite of all strategies, plans, policies which are embodied in the constitutions like national and international Cadre to look into the real picture of the child at one end for their overall development and on the other hand the Liberalisation, Privatisation and Globalisation (LPG) is becoming habeas corpus in the light of child development. Further "It shows more heat than light" on various national and international dias, which dumped thousands of tonnes upon the welfare survival and sustainable development, human dignity of child in universal and as well as in India.

REFERENCES

1. Saches Christina, 'Children's Rights: Fundamental Rights', London: Sweet and Maxwell, 1973, p. 31.
2. Sadana Ramachandran, 'Child Labour in India: Law Advocacy and Judicial Intervention', *Journal commemorating 50 years of the Indian Constitution,* 3-7 November 1999, New Delhi, p. 119.
3. World Bank, 'Globalisation and Localisation', *World Development Report* 1999-2000.
4. Abdul Aziz, 'Globalisation and Governance in India', The Hindu, May 30, 2000, p. 25.

21

SAP Human Rights and Social Justice

R.D. Vijayasekhar

Indian Constitution envisaged a positive role to the Indian State in reconstruction of the social order, protecting the political freedom and contributing to the 'gradual' transformation of the economic order. In other words it was expected to strive to build a democratic society which includes political, social and economic democracy conducive for the pursuit and promotion of human rights.

Constitution means a document having a special legal sanctity which gets out the framework and the principal functions of the organs of the Government of a State and declares the principles governing the operation of those organs. It deals with fundamental rights and Directive Principles of State Policy too. The incorporation of a formal declaration of fundamental rights in. Part III of the Constitution is deemed to be a distinguishing feature of a democratic State. These rights are prohibitions against the State. The State cannot make a law which takes away or abridges any of the rights of the citizens guaranteed in the Part III of the Constitution. If it passes such a law it may be declared unconstitutional be the courts. The Constitution has conferred on the Supreme Court the power to grant most effective remedies in the nature of writs called Habeas Corpus, mandamus, prohibition, Quo Warranto and Certiorari whenever these rights are violated. Fundamental rights are not absolute rights. They are subject to certain restrictions. Thus our Constitution tries to strike a balance between the invidiaul liberty and the social interest. The Directive Principles of State Policy in Part IV of the Constitution set out he aims and objectives to be taken up by the State in the governance of the country. Unlike the Fundamental rights, these rights are not justiciable. No action can be brought against the State against the non implementation of any provisions of Part IV. The idea of a welfare State envisaged in our Constitution can only be achieved if the States endeavour to implement them with a high sense of moral duty. Liberty, Equality and Fraternity which the Constitution seeks to secure for the people of India are to serve the primary objective of ensuring social, economic and political justice. Justice is the harmonious blending of selfish nature of man and the good of the society. The attainment of the collective goods as distinguished from individual good is the main aim of rendering justice. Combining the ideals of political, social, economic democracy with that of equality and fraternity in the Preamble, Gandhiji described as 'the India of my dream' namely-an India, in which the poorest wholly feel that it is their country in whose making they have an effective voice: an Indian in which all communities shall live in perfect harmony.[1]

The economic justice, it is obvious, was given a place of importance. The Directive Principles not only envisaged banishment of poverty by the multiplication of the National Wealth and resources but an equitable distribution thereof amongst all those who contribute towards its production.

The Article 38 requires the State to provide work for all improve the living conditions of the common man, provide sufficient food and clothing to all, provide relief for the ailing and pension for the old and infirm and educate all the children.

Article 13(1) declares that all laws in force in the territory of India immediately before the commencement of this Constitution shall be void to the extent to which they are inconsistent with the provisions of Part III of the Constitution. Clause (2) of this Article provides that the State shall not make any law which takes away or abridges the fundamental rights conferred by the Constitution and any law made in contravention of fundamental rights shall to the extent of contravention, be void. Clause (3) of this Article gives the term 'law' a very broad connotation which includes any ordiannce, order, bye-law, rule, regulation, notification, custom or usage having the force of law. Thus not only the legislative enactment, but anything mentioned here can be challenged as infringing fundamental rights.

At one time it was thought that the State was mainly concerned with the maintenance of law and order and the protection of life, liberty and property of the subject. Such a restrictive role of the State is no longer a valid concept. Today we are living in an era of a Welfare State which has to promote the prosperity and well-being of the people. The Directive Principles of State Policy lay down certain economic and social policies to be pursued by the various Governments in India, they impose certain obligation on the State to take positive action in certain directions in order to promote the welfare of the people and achieve economic democracy. Social justice and equality are complementary to each other so that both should maintain their vitality. Rule of law is a potent instrument of social justice to bring about equality.

Impact of SAP on Part IV

Article 38(a) provides that the State shall strive to promote the welfare of the people by securing and protecting as effectively as it may, a social order in which justice, social, economic and political shall inform all the institutions of national life. It would enable the State to have a national policy on wages and eliminate inequalities in various spheres of life. But SAP requires the State to undertake such activities which would result in loss of work to several workers. SAP insist on policy of privatisation. Privatisation is essential a process of creating dualism in the economy giving is to the skewed distribution of the resources and ownership of the means of production. Further, the process of globalisation fortifies ownership of foreign or multi-national companies. They are forcing for such type of liberalisation that they would have grip over certain vital means of production.

Article 41 directs the State to ensure the people within the limit of its economic capacity and development: (a) employment, (b) education and (c) public assistance in cases of employment, old age, sickness and disablement and in other cases of underserved want.

Article 45 requires the State to provide for universal literacy within 10 years after the adoption of the Indian constitution. The SAP not only would abandon the universal literacy programme but require child labour in the economy.

Article 46 enjoins the State to promote with special care the education and economic interest of the weaker sections of the people and in particular of the Scheduled Caste and Scheduled Tribes, and to protect them from social injustice and of all forms of exploitation.

Thus SAP goes against the very spirit of part IV of the constitution. It is not that the situation earlier was qualitatively better. But there were some checks in the economy and certain policy measure which were aimed in this direction. The structural adjustment requires the State to alter the very direction. Now the emphasis is on export-led growth, competition, efficiency, modernisation, technological transformation so on. 'If we consider dignified and decent life with greater equality in the society is a part of the Constitutional vision of justice, the Nation had certainly moved in a direction that is different from this vision. In fact, the recent trends forcefully indicate that it is moving exactly in the opposite direction. The Structural Adjustment is literally culmination of this draft.[2]

The entire Structural Adjustment Policy has very serious implications for the people and more so to the working class and the rural and urban poor. Quite a number of industries may have to be closed down under the criterion of efficiency and competitive ethic. The new policy also involves severe cuts on development expenditure on the welfare front, there are gong to be serious effects. The World bank instructed the government of India to reduce its buffer stocks of food grains and review its management system. They have also suggested massive cuts on subsidies which cuts into the welfare programmes. The effect can be seen on the two most vital sectors of welfare, health and education.

The constitutional vision of social justice is seriously affected under the influence of imperial needs. This will lead to a major upsurge both in the industrial and agrarian front. The SAP has no space whatsoever for a democratic handling of the situation. With the result the State inevitable will brutalised. This inverse relation between democracy and development would lead to marginalisation of the Constitution itself. Further, the crisis is far deeper as the sovereign decision making power is fast shifting from the national boundaries to international financial agencies. Thus, the SAP is setting formidable tasks-defending democracy, protecting national sovereignty, ensuring social justice.

REFERENCES

1. Gandhi, M.K. India of My Dreams, pp. 9-10.
2. Hara Gopal, G. Political Economy of Human Rights, University of Hyderabad, p. 121. *Paper submitted in the UGO National level workshop on the theme "The Rights Based Approach to Development", during 3-9, August 2002. Dept of Human Rights and Social Development, S.V. University, Tirupati.*

22

Empowerment of Agricultural Rural Women Labourers and Human Rights in the Context of Globalisation

I. Subramanyam

Women's right are human rights and should be treated as such. To quote President K.R. Narayan at the convention on Liberal values in New Delhi on January 6, 1996. "It would be seen that in the evolution of human Civilisation, Economic, Cultural, Social, Civil and Political aspects have come together to produce what are now called human rights. At the heart of the human rights lie rights and values associated with the individual human being, which in modern parlance or rather western parlance, are called liberal values, but which are inherent in every civilisation of the world."

It is the duty of the state to remove inequalities in the personal laws of various religions. Recently it has been made compulsory to include the mother's name along with that of the father in various forms required to be filled for an Indian child while seeking admission in a school and otherwise.

Women constitute atleast one third of the country's economically active population, particularly in the unorganised sector. Low literacy levels, skill based and knowledge grounded technologies along with patriarchal social control restrain women's access to resource which might enable them to equip themselves to meet the challenges and take advantage of the opportunities provided by the new economic policy. A culturally steeped social and economic life is not conducive to a gender neutral wage policy.

Agricultural labourers, who constitute nearly 70 percent of total rural labour households, suffer from seasonal unemployment, job insecurity, poverty, indebtedness, bondage, migration, inability to get statutory minimum wages, illiteracy, malnourishment, lack of access to assets like cultivated land, discrimination and incapability to from or join any organisation.

Since the agricultural rural women labourers do not have fixed employees relation as most of them work either as casual labourers or as contract labourers, they are not entitled for any protective social security benefits, which their counterparts get in industries the process of macro economic contraction (eg. lower public sector investment in farm and social sectors) and reduction in development role of the state, initiated during (1991) and thereafter, have actually worsened their economic condition. The qualitative restrictions lifted from agricultural products and attempt to dismantle PDS may have adverse impact on agricultural growth, which can result in reducing labour demand, leading to further deterioration in the condition of agricultural labour.

An important indicator of well being of agricultural labourers in the magnitude of real wages receive by them. As per the 55th rounds NSS, RWs of casual agricultural labourers in 1999-2000 was only Rs. 25.48 per day per male, which is much lower than the average of MWs of 14 states (average being Rs. 44.13 per day). This indicates that minimum wages Act has not been implemented effectively.

Although the average wage rate of both male and female have increased in real terms during the last five years, the growth is lowest among all rural activities. Thus, in spite of absolute rise in their wages, their position vis-a-vis their counterparts in other activities in both rural and urban areas have actually deteriorated.

Shrinking Opportunities

Gross Value Added per worker in agriculture has grown by 3.3 per cent per annum between 1993-94 and 1999-2000. The number of persons employed per 1000 population in rural areas declined from 444 to 417 and unemployment rate increased in case of rural male and females from 56 and 67 respectively in 1993-94 to 72 and 73 respectively in 1999-2000. It shows clearly that in spite of fairly high GDP growth rate during this period, then was sharp decline in rural employment. The average number of days the rural male workers worked dropped from 331 days per annum in 1993-94 to 327 days per annum in 1999-2000. However, is the average umber of days the rural females workers worked increased from 241 to 246 during the same period. The increasing number of females work days reveals that the income earned by males were not adequate enough to support the family and females were compelled to work more to compensate for the meager income earned by their male counterparts.

Existing Provisions

Social security to agricultural labourers is the responsibility of both the Centre and State governments as it is enlisted in this concurrent list of the India constitution. Although, Constitution of India has made provision to safeguard the interest of weaker sections, little has been done so far in this direction. Article 41 of the constitution under Directive principles of State Policy says, "The State shall, with in the limits of its economic capacity and development make effective provision for securing the right to work, to education and to public assistance in case of unemployment, oldage, sickness and disablement, and in other cases on under severed wants". However, even after 50 years planned development, state could not provide effective social safety net to poor workers.

During 1997, the then government prepared a comprehensive agricultural workers Bill to guarantee minimum wage and better working conditions. Sadly, several governments crane in after that but the bill could not be passed in Parliament.

In Andhra Pradesh the situation of women in terms of literacy status is not very encouraging , as 66 per cent of them are still illiterate Women worker are largely concentrated in the unorganised sector particularly in the agricultural sector, ecomprising of a formidable 88 per cent. The figure includes both cultivators and agricultural labourers in the unorgansied sector Women participate in all major agricultural operations which include preparation of land, sowing of seeds, transplanting, weeding, harvesting, winnowing, preparation of compost and manure pits, application of manure, spraying of pesticides and insecticides, storage of seeds and food grains. Majority of this work is not only time consuming but also strenuous. Hence, it leads to further depletion of the already scarce resources of the female worker. This is turn has an adverse impact on her health condition.

Due to globalisation the Indian agriculture has adopted new technology to tolerate its competitiveness in the production. This affects the Rural Agricultural Labourers workdays and violates the right to work. The rural labourers migrated to near by urban areas like towns and cities for construction works and other jobs. As discussed above especially the agricultural rural women not in a position to live in their native villages.

23

Capital Centric Development-Patriarch Chain of Capital, State and Households—The Question of Unfreedoms

Dr. M. Vanamala

Women in general suffer different forms of disadvantages (unfreedoms) and threats to basic human rights in the socio-economic and household spheres. These unfreedoms reinforce each other. The State, the capital and the household contribute to these unfreedoms at their own levels. These trends form a chain in a market/capital centric/patrichal transitional society like India. As the 'New Industrial Policy' is moving more and more towards the new world order which is capital centric and embedded in inequalities (Amartya Sen, 1999). The unfreedoms are getting intensified. Therefore the protection of human rights in general and that of female rights in particular need a critical evaluation.

The 1991 industrial policy which has been formulated under unregulated, liberalised market conditions, unlike the earlier policies which were guided by protected system, the implications are far more serious. The policy implications for employment are very critical for protection of human rights as it is insensitive to the basic livelihood of the majority people who are concentrated in rural areas and dependent on primary sector for livelihood. The high pressure of surplus labour on limited area of land for their own cultivation is a basic reason for its 'zero' (low) marginal productivity. This vulnerability of the peasants has been further aggravated by new policy by encouraging unregulated migration. The resulted in further swelling of labour in local areas where the new industries were set up. This adversely affected the bargaining power of labour in general and that of female labour in particular as the female labour has limited freedom for mobility. These strategic logistic of new industries1 are discussed in this paper with the help of an empirical study.

Unless the society attempts to ward off these inequalities and aggregated 'unfreedoms' over the years (Amrtya Sen, 1999), it is impossible to realise equality resulting in rights for women. The "un-freedoms" are spread over socio economic and household spheres of her life. The inequalities or the 'social un-freedoms' like unequal educational opportniteis[2] unequal nutritional standards, poor health standards, and survival capabilities curtail her freedom. Curtailment of freedoms are curtailment of her fuller participation in economic sector. In the economic sphere women face 'lack of liberty' to engage in the sale of her labour power (Amrtya Sen, 1999). Such 'lack of liberty' or 'unfreedoms' like, gendered division of labour, forced, repetitive, undignified, un-remunerative and unskilled low status labour, hazardous labour involving long hours of work exploit female labour. The un-freedoms at the household level are her constant subjugation and drudgery, constant domestic work and child bearing curtail her creative abilities resulting in suppression of her social opportunities in a wide range of domain (Jean Dreze and Amartya Sen, 2001). All these factors leading to vulnerable conditions for women consequent to industrialisation in 90s and resulting in loss of female rights over employment across class, caste, gender, patriarchy, capital, State and labour are discussed in this paper.

This study attempts the changes in the nature and quality of employment both in the agricultural and industrial sector consequent to industrialisation. For this purpose case studies of a village and female labour situation in a manufacturing industry are selected. To analyse changes in female employment these case studies focus on some of the specific human rights stated in the Articles 23, 24 and 25 of the Indian Constitution.

Theoretical Discourse

It is argued that directly or indirectly all the activities a woman does contribute to capital accumulation in a capitalist oriented development. The household chores entail familial relations and shape economic relations, which in turn contribute to capital accumulation. The roles of female in reproduction and maintenance of labour force reinforces reproduction of the specific social relations and paves the way for capital accumulation. This includes one; looking after or caring for well-being of her husband and children; two; the sexual division of labour of the capitalist system coupled with patriarchal family, perpetuate the economic subordination; three: distinguishing production for use from production for exchange, gives rise to production for use in the *'private world of home'* and *'female labour'* and production for exchange is increasingly done outside the home with the male labour. It is held that 'the production of use values, contributed for women are under *'non-wage relation of production'* with in the capitalist mode of production. Such contribution of women is a *necessary precondition for the reproduction of capital and* remains *"invisible"* from the point of view of capital (Althusser, 1971a)[3]. This fits into the argument that this type of dependency and exploitation gets expanded with extended dimensions of capital (Marx, 1976). Marx (1976) and Engels argued that capitalist mode of production led to class formation which in turn led to hierarchical relation between sexes in the family. The following diagram presents this pattern.

Surplus Value Generated by Women's Productive and Reproductive Role in the family

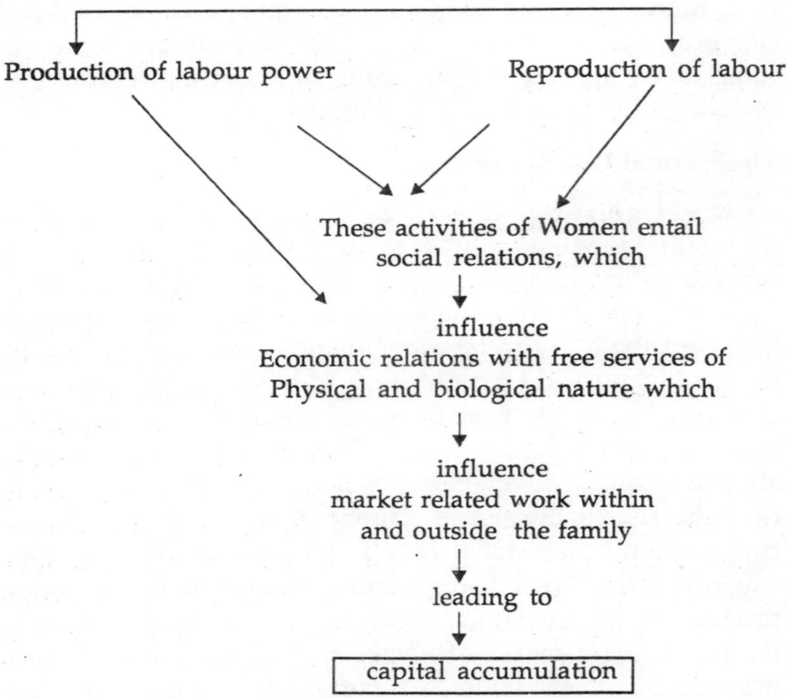

It is this pattern that the case study of the village sought to discuss.

Case Study of a Village

In this part the female employment[4] during 90s, in a village 'Muttangi' is presented. The village is located in a backward district 'Medak' (Andhra Pradesh, India), 40 kilometres away from Hyderabad city. The District Medak was selected during 70s as Lok sabha Constituency by Mrs. Indira Gandhi (Prime Minister). This was the period when political agenda, of "Gareebi Hatao (Eradicte Poverty) was brought to the forefront. This region was specially selected for industrialisation under 'the policy for development of backward region'. The main focus of the industrial policy was 'growth with Social justice'. The village under study also saw industrialisation in the second phase during 90s in the wake of new industrial policy with a thrust on unregulated, free market and liberalised economy. The village lost a lot of cultivable land. People had to find alternative survival tasks. The following sample has been selected to study the new livelihood tasks and their impact on women.

Table—1: Total no of sample households selected (caste wise) out of aggregate

	1979			*1989*					*1999*
caste	*a no*	*sampl*	*%3/2*	*a no*	*sample*	*%6/5*	*a no*	*sample*	*%9/10*
1	2	3	4	5	6	7	8	9	10
SC	46	46	100	69	43	62.3	95	27	28.42
BC	171	171	100	257	149	57.97	302	78	25.82
FC	63	63	100	94	42	44.6	136	34	25.00
Total	280	280	100	420	234	55.7	533	139	26.07

"a no" refers to aggregate number of households in the village: 3/2, 65, 9/10 are column numbers. The data on the total households is collected from gram panchayat records.

The sample households selected comprise more than 26 percent of the aggregate in the villages (table1) and forms a representative sample. The sample members from each of the households are drawn to cover traditional and modern occupations, livelihood tasks, skilled and unskilled activities to form a representative multistaged, purposive, stratified random sample. This coverage is done keeping in view the structural factors of caste, class and gender (table 2). Participatory observation and questionnaire methods are used to elicit the data.

Table 2: Total household members covered in the sample

	1979				1989		1999
caste	*a no*	*female*	*%*	*male*	*female*	*male*	*female*
SC	82	75		61	82	83	80
BC	263	244		251	249	230	199
FC	145	98		74	78	104	86
Total	489	417		386	409	417	365

Note: The number is brackets are % in vertical totals.

IV

Impact of Patriachy

The following responses of women explain the hold of patriachy on women's life at the Household level, in industrial front, in the state policies and in women themselves. The patriarchy in the industry is evident from the fact that they did not offer justified work to women. The patriarchy in the state is too obvious from the fact that it has put no efforts for development of work opportunities for women. The patriarchy within women are evident from their value system that 'if sufficient income is earned by spouse they need not work for income' (vanamala, 1998). These dimensions can be explained with the help of the following responses of women.

From the data in table (3) it is evident that as high as 22 percent prefer to work at home. This is because entire household responsibility is treated to be that of women

Table—3: Responses of Women for Not Earning Income (multiple responses)

	SC	*BC*	*FC*	*Total*	%
Secure job for husband/son with higher income	13	12	16	41	14.85
Wage work is not allowed by husband and elders as children are young	9	9	9	27	9.78
Do only household work	6	28	26	60	21.73
Work only on own land	1	5	12	18	6.52
Do only agricultural work	3	10	4	17	6.15
Forward castes do not do wage work	nil	5	13	18	6.52
Women from certain BC castes* do not do wage work	nil	12	nil	12	4.3
Do not have necessary skills and education	7	24	10	41	14.85
Interested to work in government sector	1	1	2	4	1.44
Interested to do business, no capital	nil	7	3	10	3.62
Want to work in the industry but industries prefer male to female	5	6	2	13	4.7
Total	47	128	101	276	100.00

which renders her mobility difficult. This could be the reason why they feel that work should be available at home. Another 15 percent held that their spouses and sons are earning sufficient income. About 10 percent expressed that they cannot take up any outside work as their children are very young. About seven per cent of the respondents preferred to work on their own fields. In all these responses work out to almost 52 percent and indicate the strong hold of different forms of patriarchal values in the society.

It is not easy for those women who want to work. As the difference in the education and skills along with class, caste and gender play a significant role in finding out suitable sources of livelihood. The following table presents the differences in education and skills among male and female in the village across castes.

The data on over all educational levels in the village (table 3) suggest that illiteracy extends to 33 percent of sample members. The overall educational attainments show that about 22 percent have completed primary education, 38 percent studied between 6th and 10th classes. Those who have completed intermediate and gradation comprise mere six and two percent respectively.

The differences in educational attainments of male and female across castes is striking. The female illiteracy among SCs and BCs is double to that of the male illiteracy. The illiteracy of women among FCs is five times to that of illiteracy of the male. The female illiterates in the total respective female sample persists to the extent of 49, 48 and 31 per cent across SC[5]s, BCs, and FCs respectively.

The data on female education from primary level to intermediate level shows that the percentage of the female educated is not significantly lower to that of percentage of the male (table 3). In contrast there is a sudden jump in the differences at the higher education levels. The

Table—4: Education particulars of the sample members (1999)

Qualification	*SC*				*BC*				*FC*				*Total Per%*		
	Male	*Per*	*Female*	*Per*	*Male*	*Per*	*Female*	*·Per*	*Male*	*Per*	*Female*	*Per*	*No.*	*%*
Illiterates	21.00 (27.20)	10.09	36.00 (48.60)	17.30	52 (27.5)	25.00	75 (48.0)	36.05	5 (6.17)	2.40	19 (30.6)	9.13	208	32.55
Primary Per%	15.00 (19.40)	10.86	9.00 (12.10)	6.52	47 (24.8)	34.05	32.00 (20.5)	23.8	21 (25.9)	152	14 (22.5)	10.14	138	21.59
6-10 per%	(34.00 (44.1)	13.9	25.00 (33.70)	10.2	70 (37.00)	28.68	42 (26.90)	17.21	47 (58.00)	19.26	26 (41.90)	10.65	244	38.18
Intermediate	3.00 (3.89)	8.33	3.00 (4.05)	8.37	17 (8.99)	47.22	6 (3.84)	16.66	5 (61.7)	13.88	2 (3.22)	5.55	36	6.65
Graduation Per %	4.00 (5.19)	30.76	(1.35)	1.00	7.69 (1.58)	3	23.07 (0.64)	1	7.69 (3.70)	8	23.07 (1.61)	!7.69	18.	2.03
Total	77	12.05	74	11.58	189	29.57	156	24.41	181	12.67	62	9.70	639	100.00

Source: Collected from field by the author
The numbers in parenthesis are percentages of vertical totals

percentage of the graduated among men constitute four times in SCs and three times in both of BCs and FCs to that of women graduates. Among the female BCs less than one percent and among SCs and FCs one and two percents respectively could complete graduation. It explains that attainment of higher education by women in negligible irrespective of caste[5] background. This explains that female education continues to be neglected in the overall social system more so among SCs, despite the reservations and educational support from the state.

About the skills attained by women (table 5) also show dismal picture. It is to be noted that 75 per cent of the female workforce is unskilled and engaged in agricultural labour work. The traditional caste based skills like cane work and pot making continue among only BCs. In the traditional skilled activities like cane work and pot making women constitute 31 and six percent of the total female sample. These skills are imparted through traditional practices without formal training. Therefore these skills are invisible in the formal sense of the term. The price fixed for the products based on these skills is low. Further the activities based on these skills in the village are home based and are considered as subsidiary occupations indicating the lower level income yielding from them.

The women who possess modern skills like printing and tailoring constitute six and fifty six per cent respectively in the total female workforce. Although these skills are imparted through formal training, they do not fetch much of income as these women carry out that work at home. Home based stitching is considered as unskilled work. Further there are no opportunities for women for up gradation of skills. The upper caste women cannot accept clothes from lower castes for stitching. It is considered below dignity for upper castes. All these factors effect their demand factor. Hence the women tailors are forced to accept lower wages for their tailoring. This trend explain

Table—5: Skill particulars of sample household members (1999)

	SC		*BC*		*FC*		*Total*	
	Male	*Female*	*Male*	*Female*	*Male*	*Female*	*Male*	*Female*
Skills								
Cane work	nil	nil	14	5	nil	nil	14 (16.86)	5 (31.25)
Potter	nil	nil	21		nil	nil	2 (2.40)	1 (6.25)
Tailoring	1	1	4	4	1	4	6 (7.22)	9 (56.25)
Printing and painting	nil	nil-	2	nil	1	1	3 (3.61)	1 (6.25)
Mason	2		2				4 (4.30)	nil
Machine operator	1	nil	3	nil	10	nil	14 (16.86)	nil
Driving	1		7		2		10 (12.04)	nil
Technical	7		15		8		30	nil
Total work force	13	14	58	41	22	9	83	16

that The skills acquired by women formal or informal if enmeshed with household activities, they loose their visibility and value.

It is further observed that this type of home based exchange activity brings down the prices of the market based production that is the prices of male tailoring outside home as women turn into competitor for male tailors.

About the skill levels among the male (table 5), the data reveals that more than 32 per cent of men are technicians and about 15 per cent are operators. The above differences in the skill levels between the male and the female have far reaching implications to women. Women are forced to take up manual work while male take up mental, skilled, technical, challenging work resulting in higher remunerations. The nature of employment and earning of women invariably lower. Her earnings are considered as supplementary. The superiority of mental work over physical relegates women to lower status. Consequently women become subordinate and subservient in the household power relations.

The caste wise data reveals that a majority of the male FCs are in mechanical and operator category. These activities are modern and fetch more income. While a majority of BCs are engaged in the activities that fetches lesser income. However driving is a new activity in which SCs and BCs have entered.

The trends show that the industrialisation helped the upper caste male to acquire technical and skilled knowledge. It has had no significant impact on female particularly on lower caste women. The class, caste and gender gaps have been further reinforced and strengthened by the process of industrialisation. The following discussion brings out these factors.

The Process of Exclusion

Breverman, (1976) argued that the process of industrialisation "deskills" the workers. The process of de-skilling or the process of exclusion is noticed with the loss of land and industrialisation around the village under study. In the decade of 70s the hired labour in agriculture sector was one of the predominant occupations. This has declined between 1979 ad 1999 from 47 percent to 13 percent. The female workers working on their own land came down in the total work force from 20 percent in 1999. Between 1979 and 1999 the types of occupations available for women have gone down from 16 to nine. This marked decline in alternatives employment initiated deskilling of the workers.

This could be seen in the process that when agricultural production fell due to loss of land, the cattle used in agriculture automatically got reduced. These changes affected the demand for cane baskets which were used extensively in removing animal dung, for feeding animal, for lifting agricultural produce, preserving and agricultural produce and seeds for next crop, for saving, cleaning grains, using for carts and for agricultural and social rituals. The industries around introduced the culture of 'plastic and steel substitutes'. Added to this when bullocks are sold off by the peasants transport became problem for getting the cane from forest. All these factors affected adversely resulting in deskilling of cane work. The skills in pottery also got deskilled when the steel and aluminium vessels substituted the pottery.

The occupation like wool spinning disappeared totally on account of conversion of agricultural land into real estate. The shift of land from agriculture resulted in reduction of demand for rearing of goats and sheep which was largely used for the purpose of fertilisation of land. This demand also went down with the decrease in the grazing land for these animals. Water pollution aggravated the problem. This resulted in disappearance of sheep and goat rearing, followed by spinning activity. There is no determined effort for alternative skill formation.

The caste based service activity like 'washing' (dhobi), changed its form and context. The washer women stopped collection of clothes from clientele houses for washing. This has happened primarily because households got tap water connections which made washing easy. Secondly the male members of the households could set up 'dhobi kits' in business center. The work got shifted from female to male. These are trends of "exclusion" and "masculanisation". They are common when overall employment avenues are declining. Thus women lost their palace in the traditional occupations without finding alternative employment. However women still continue with this activity when there are activities associated with birth, death and puberty in the household. This is "dirty work" done by washer women symbolizing low of status.

The overall evidence suggests that when 'new industries' are set up in a particular region many households in and around the villages the industrial area got uprooted from traditional occupations (Vanamala, 2000). The uprooted majority of male members preferred only work in industries. While women could not exercise their option as poverty forced then to opt for some work at any level of income. The industries also created marginal opportunities for women. The following data shows the number of women who could enter the industries from the village.

From the above data (table 6) it is too obvious that industrialisation would have varied impact on men and women as their work opportunities differ. The following are instances that further reinforce the trends.

Table—6: Male and Female working in the industries

	Sample size in '99	*Actual no of industrial workers*	*% in '99 sample*
Male	417	171	41.00
Female	365	8	2.19
Total	782	179	22.89

A young woman mentioned that her husband and his all who are all educated brothers could take up industrial work which was meant for educated unemployed. With the result the pot making work could be taken by women. But she did not have the pot making tools. Her in-laws owned them. All the women in the family (wives of all brothers) used them for a day in a week. The in-laws claimed a share from their earnings. She lamented that banks were not coming forward to sanction a loan for purchase of such tools. This prevents all of them from fully enjoying fruits of their hard labour.

Another trend of impact of industrialisation is that majority of women remained 'idle' as they could not find suitable work and were forced to become "housewives" despite of their inclination to work and the dire necessity to work on account of their poverty. Thus women lost their basic right to livelihood.

The changes in the nature of female employment consequent to industrialisation brought changes in household power relations, followed by changes in women's quality of economic life. The field data shows that the female activities which are considered "difficult to measure" (Indira hirway, 02) such as the household chores, home based production, caste based and home based occupations, subsistence cultivation on own land, 'exchange services' in cultivation have increased in the village. These activities generate economic values but uncounted for the market purpose. Hence they are invisible, unpaid. These activities do not contribute to free and dignified living of women.

The Process of Inclusion

The process of "Inclusion" is a complex and differentiated process across class, caste, gender and patriarchy. A section of the women who are confined to their own household work are forced to take up home based work like dairy and tailoring as the wages paid by industries to their spouses are very low and the nature of employment is uncertain, flexible, informal and casual. The male members of the family think that milk business is a suitable occupation for the housewife to support the regular family income. Hence many presently casual industrial workers sold their cultivable and to buy milch cattle. This resulted in a change in the nature and pattern of female work. The household drudgery considerably went up. They have to manage the regular household chores along with dairy activity. The dairy involves cleaning of sheds, animals, fetching of gross and grazing item outside. Women who have shifted their occupation from cultivation to home based, lost the privilege of working outside the home with other workers. They got secluded and "domesticated".[6]

As has been already mentioned the home based tailoring is another such activity taken by some of the housewives. This activity of women fetches very meager income to female compared to the non-home based tailoring done by male. It is very important to note that the home based tailoring pulls down the entire tailoring business itself. This is because the female tailors are compelled to charge lower rates on account of their lower skills in tailoring. Thus women experienced disadvantages for not having created proper employment opportunities.

The home based activities do not distinguishing between exchange value and value for domestic use, and between skilled and unskilled (physical and household) activities. This makes measurement of production value difficult and the activities invisible. Hence they are not considered for the purpose of policy planning. Another implication of "domestication"[7] is that some women are forced to take up multiple activities due to compulsions of survival, as income generated from a single survival task is not sufficient for their livelihood. For instance the field data shows that some of the women took up dairy and caste based occupations along with agriculture and household chores. This forced[8] and compulsory labour affected their health (mental and physical) adversely.

The employment of women as stone cutters explains the "inclusion" trends. The massive construction work consequent to industrialisation created employment for women as cheap labour. This shows that women are employed more as their labour is exploited as higher levels.

The data on employment of women in industries shows that mere two percent of the women got opportunity to work in the industries. This is partly because industries preferred migrant (Female) employees. For the first time in the year 1999, 18 women from the sample stated that they are unemployed. These are the qualified women willing to work in the industries. The opportunities are lacking. They also feel that industries do not prefer women. They want to work in the industries as they are educated and think that the work in industries is light, regular better and more income earning. But these women are recruited in unsecure, unskilled undignified manual work without any regard to their educational qualifications.

However the data relating to a fraction of women who are working in the industries from the village, shows that their overall conditions have not changed much despite their employment in new economic activity. This is because the reforms are implemented in an iniquitous social structure Unequal distribution of assets and opportunities rooted in the socio-economic structure has largely influenced the process of industrialisation and its overall impact. Therefore the reforms have increased the inequalities already existing between caste and gender.

Domestic Violence

The values of inequalities in an unequal society are reinforced and perpetuated by the State, the capital and the households. The study obseves that at household level the domestic labour and child caring in the village continues to be totally women's responsibility. The burden of looking after children and domestic work locks up women in the classical domestic division of labour.

The values of inequalities are also evident from the undignified living conditions of women in the family. For instance kitchen (where only women works) is located outside slabbed rooms in majority of the working class households to protect the house from firewood smoke. This kitchen is a thatched hut with low roof without side walls and placed by the side of cattle shed. These houses also have no bath room facility and are not connected with sanitation and protected water lines.[9] These people also cannot afford individual connections. Thus the people of these households particularly women are experiencing unhygienic and undignified living conditions. Added to it there are no medical facilities in the village. The villagers believe the witchraft as cause for their ill health. The midwifery is still in practice for maternity cases. These factors resulted in unequal male female ratio in the village 91.57:1).

It is observed that the migration of working class into village caused serious crisis in martial relations in the many households. The practice of bigany and prostitution became (are) more common among these classes. The liquor consumption has gone up several times. The crisis is also observed in parting with the income for household expenditure. All these developments show that poverty conditions persist rendering dignity and freedom of working class women problematic.

Secondly, the new industrial policy could not sustain the productive activity in rural areas. As has already been mentioned in has promoted the 'rent-seeking' phenomenon. The households converted productive asset—land—into speculative and rental business which neither generated employment nor income to the landless. The 'self-help' program introduced by government as alternative employment also ended up as rent seeking activity. The rent seeking activities lead to trends like increase in dowry rate and contribute to deterioration of female status and dignity. This is one of the consequences of overall increase in land prices.

It is observed that strategically the industries preferred migrant labour over local labour. This created surplus labour in the region and weakened their bargaining power. This has set reverse wage spiral both in agriculture and industrial sector. Women are hit as they are more vulnerale for want of mobility.

The processes like 'casualisation', 'contractualsiation', and 'distress employment' are observed in the village. These trends witnessed are common in both agricultural and industrial sectors. They adversely effect the labour in general and female labour in particular, as they are compelled to take up work for low wage to keep the households fed. It is to be specially noted that mere earnings do not ensure security to women what is important is the freedom to enjoy those earnings as that alone gives the real security and status.

Fifthly, the unregulated input markets lead to increased input costs. The families with more number of female labour have leased-in cultivable land from landed households. This is one form of unpaid family labour. It neither promotes freedom of access to her earnings nor promotes her status and dignity.

Some more trends are observed in the village, which adversely effect the households. The processes like 'unprotected tenancy', 'landed labour', 'depeasantisation' 'group-contracts'[9] (specially of women) "Housewifisation" and "Domestication"[10] have hit the women in the village. The overall changes indicate that the vulnerability of the households has been increasing particularly of female work force.

Case Study of a Manufacturing Industry

Reforms have led to the rapid expansion of the informal sector. The main objective of the industries set up under deregualted and liberalised market system is obviously to make quick profits to become 'a world class company'. In pursuit of this objective these industries introduced changes in their organisational, managerial, technological and operational set up. These changes are so designed that they prefer low skills, female workers and opt for informalisation and segmented employment. Some of these jobs are contractual, casual, insecure, flexible, result in informal work relations. This is called 'low road flexible' employment strategy which causes vicious downward-spiralling effect. As 94 percent of female workers are engaged in work in the informal jobs, female workers are more hard hit by these market changes. This is in addition to the fact that traditionally the wages of female workers have been fixed lower than the male workers in male dominated informal industries.

The industry's recruitment system coupled with prescribed pre-requites for the workers to get qualified for recruitment are very tactical. For instance the nature of employment is made on hierarchical and segmented basis. The industry does not employ female employees on the management side including the supervisory levels. The female workers are appointed only on the operation side at the tail end of the production process. This segmentation increases vulnerability of the workers and management's stranglehold over workers. The arrangement of the workers or work division in *'process lines'* is mainly designed from the cost-effective angle. The machines are operated by workers in a *multiple-machines-operation-system.* This entails flexibilisation, informalisation of work relations and causalisation of employment which together lead to maximisation of vulnerability of workers.

The working conditions in the industry are exploitative. The girls recruited are young between the age group of 16 to 17 years and they have to carry out the operations for eight to sixteen hours in a standing position. These girls do not have usual household responsibilities as they are with their parents. The latter provide shelter, health care and other support to these dependent daughters. Thus these industrial units are heavily subsidised in an indirect form by the families of these female workers. Parents of these workers want their daughter to earn to contribute to the expenditure of marriage. This vulnerability of the families provided the industry with the supply of surplus cheap labour. Vulnerability of these workers is also more on account of their migration status and lack of local support. There are hardly any social security measures. All this has not resulted in any resistance for better working conditions.

The industry resorted to several manoeuvres for deterring the workers from organising. It has segregated them in terms of nature of employment, wages, annual increments, and system of wage payment. There is also a difference in the non wage benefits like PF, LIC, leaves etc. The management has also introduced such an evaluation system which leaves no scope for workers either to interact or organise. The division of labourers creates conditions where loyalty and obedience are the criterion for performance.

It is significant to note that in-spite-of the industry earning profit, it is resorting to rapid informalisation practices resulting in expansion of causal workers. It is adopting the "JIT" and "Demand Pull" techniques to reduce expenditure on inventories. These techniques in-turn generate OT work. The industry has replaced the system of double payment for OT work to trainees with the provision of casual leave (c-off). All these lead to mass scale casualisation, insecure work conditions and lower wages. The flexibility that is built in the industry coupled with the surplus labour supply in the market rendered the workers in general and women workers in particular extremely vulnerable. The State which ought to have provided better working conditions as a part of its national and international commitment has been indifferent to these trends. This is in spite of the fact that the state provides several incentives in addition to subsidies in the name of industrial development in backward region. On the whole this study reveals that the forms of extraction of surplus are changing more to the disadvantage of workers in general and female workers in particular.

Conclusions

The study of impact of industrialisation on the rights of women indicates that the household work of cooking, cleaning and child care continue to be entirely women's responsibility. This led them to look for work available at home itself. This also explains in a large way the hold of partiarchy on women. A further enquiry reveals that there are differences in the formation of educational and skill levels across the gender and castes. The data on male and female education shows that the differences are marginal up to intermediate level but as we move to higher levels the percentage of women who completed higher education are found to be insignificant.

The analysis of skills acquired shows that they are acquired more by male than female. The skills acquired by women shows the same pathetic state of their development. Further the skills acquired by women with formal or informal training are considered as unskilled. This compelled women to accept more of manual, repetitive and low status work. She is forced to accept lower incomes. Women work in the house enmeshed the production activity with household work. Therefore home based activity earns lesser income compared to non-home based activity of male. The study reveals that forward cases are in the higher income earning activities.

The overall trends show that industrialisation helped upper castes, male to acquire skills and technical knowledge. It has had no significant impact on female particularly on lower caste women. These practices have widened the existing gaps between castes and gender.

The study also reveals the *exclusion* and *inclusion* processes. Hired labour and labour on own land declined. The number of occupations available for women has declined after 90s. The activities like wool spinning vanished indicating deskilling of rural artisans. The caste service such as dhobi went down.

From the uprooted families male wanted to work only in the industries despite the insecurity of the job. The burden of survival of families increasingly fell on women particularly during *no income period* of the male. This trend forced women to accept any work at any income yielding level. Added to this industries created marginal work opportunities to women. All these trends have had varied impact on men and women. The overall trends show that women were not enjoying the fruits of their hard labour. Several women remained idle and forced to become housewives despite their inclination and dire need to work on account of their poverty.

The nature of process of *inclusion* shows that most of the activities taken up by women are not *visible, unaccounted, earns meagre income and involves long hours of work.* Women are taking up these activities within the household enmeshed with domestic work. Dairy and tailoring are such activities noticed in the village. A majority of the women are forced to take up multiple activities as income from a single activity is not sufficient for survival. This forced and compulsory work affected women's health.

It is noted that women are employed more to reduce the expenditure on production than enlarging avenues for employment. For this reason women were recruited in *insecure lower status jobs. Multi-machine-operation* system is practised in the industries. Industries are heavily subsidised in an indirect form by the families of the female workers. Therefore, the overall conditions of women working even in the industries have not changed. The broad trends show that the industrialisation has been influenced by the iniquitous socio-economic conditions and it has also reinforced the existing structure.

This continuity of the structure could be seen in the domestic conditions and it has also reinforced the existing structure.

This continuity of the structure could be seen in the domestic front. The study noticed that the problems of inequalities continued. Women lived undignified living conditions. Immigration created serious crisis in martial relations. All these developments show that poverty conditions persist rendering dignity and freedom of working class women problematic.

Both the case studies reveal that a constructive state intervention is necessary for the protection of women from becoming vulnerable to market and in the protection of her rights. The state intervention in the spheres of facilitating access to productive assets to overcome the problems of exploitation. There has to be an initiative to impart alternative skills to women along with strengthening educational accessibility. Efforts to bringing attitudinal changes in the society as a whole and in rural women in particular has to be recognised. There has to be social space for mobilsiation of women which would help in protection of rights of women.

REFERENCES

1. Braverman Harry (1974) *Labour and Monopoly Capital: The Degradation of Work in the Twentieth Century,* Monthly Review Press, New York and London. Papola Alakh N. Sharma (1999) *Gender and Employment in India Indian* Society of Labour Economic, IEG, Friedrich Ebert Stiflung, Vikas Publishing House Pvt. Ltd.

2. Sonpar Shobhana Kapur Ravi (2001) *Non-Conventional Indicators Gender Disparities Under Strucural Reforms,* EPW Jan 6 Vol xxxvi no. 1 Vanamala (1995) Industrialisation impact on rural women, Indian political Economy Association Fourth Conference Department of Economics University of Hyderabad, 20-22 Jan. Vijay *New Townships* (2000) unpublished paper.

3. New industries refer to the industries set up under new policy, in liberalised, unregulated market economy. See Vijay G. 'New Industrial Townships' an unpublished paper.

4. Amartya Sen argues that literacy enriches capability of a (wo)men. It helps to process any information, to reflect, deal with other people, to chose more freely and freedom to chose her life.

5. Hutchinson of London, (NA) "Women Take Issues" Women Studies Group, Center fro Contemporary Cultural Studies University of Birmingham.

6. Between 1993-94 and 1999-2000 there was a decline in agricultural workers, it wast below 60 per cent and there was an absolute reduction in the number of women workers in rural India (see Sundaram K. Special Article Employment-Unemployment situation in Nineties, some results from NSS 55th Round Survey, EPW March 17, 2001).

7. It is observed that in Andhra Pradesh a substantial decline in the percentage share of wage-paid employment was associated with an equally significant increase in the percentage share of self-employment. Another important trend in the state is that the gender differentials in daily real wage in non-agricultural occupations widened (see Sharma 2001, IJLE, Vol 44 no1).

8. These castes are Sara, Bhatraju, Gandla, Thammali, Padmasali.

9. Inspite the reservation policy the percentage of SC female literate is lesser than the percentage of male literate.

10. This concept refers to taking production work into home.

11. Pushing the productive work into home.

12. This is against the convention of abolition of forced labour.

13. The effluents let out from the industries polluted surface and ground water. The Pollution Control Board noted this region under 'Red alert, danger zone' indicating that the water from

this region is not useful for use. The Supreme Court ordered the state to supply drinking water to village under this zone for free of cost. But the water authorities are collecting the water less charges. These charges are exceeding the total revenue amount of the village. Women whoever wants to work join in the 'village group' to participate in the contract work. Group members distribute the wages paid for the contract work. It is observed that women were getting mere Rs. two per head and two hours work. It is observed that women were getting Rs. Two per head, work was available for two hours.

14. This refers to the process of pushing productive work into home.

